Wind from the Sea
Essays in Redemptive Education

Amy E. Imbody

Amy E. Imbody

Edited by Heidi Poniatowski

Designed by Erica Reiter

Cover: Student artwork from Trace Academy, Orlando, FL

The Center for Redemptive Education
Lantern Light Press
Ashland, VA USA

ISBN: 1986179893
ISBN-13: 978-1986179898

Dedicated to Redemptive Educators everywhere.

Amy E. Imbody

CONTENTS

Amy E. Imbody

INTRODUCTION

Jesus' Pedagogy

In the brief span of Jesus' teaching career, He demonstrated a simple approach to pedagogy and curriculum. He took whatever was at hand, whatever was before Him, whatever experience was familiar and accessible, and He used these, along with God's Word, to bring light and understanding where there had been shadow and unknowing. I find He continues to take this same approach with me: using whatever is at hand, whatever is before me, and all that He allows me to experience - in conjunction with His Word - to bring light and understanding to *my* "shadows" and "unknowing." The essays in this book are my response to some of these lessons. In turn, I share them with you, as I have shared them with many, in the hope that together we can continue to learn from Him even as we teach our children at home and at school.

Most, if not all, of the essays can serve as a starting place for important thinking and dialogue. Asking ourselves and one another (and the Lord!), "What does this show me? What questions does it provoke? What application can I make to my own practice as an educator in response to these ideas?" will yield plenty to digest. With that degree of simplicity, anyone can make use of this book, reading it either as an individual or within a community of learners, to discover and develop an approach to education that is BRIE: Biblical, Relational, Integral and Experiential. Each essay is brief, designed for already-busy teachers, parents, grandparents, administrators. An easy-prep way to organize study is to assign the reading of one essay per week, asking each participant to create one discussion question for each week's gathering. Obviously, a group may find a bi-weekly or monthly discussion to be optimal. The point is that the only thing required is to read, to wonder, to be ready to discuss.

Blessings on your Redemptive Education explorations through the pages of this book. I would love to hear about your adventures! Write to me at amy.imbody@RedemptiveEducation.org and share your own stories and lessons from the quest to align with God's design for teaching and learning: Redemptive Education.

1 EXPLORERS

"My leaf won! My leaf won!" a sixth-grade boy shouts. His buddies high-five him and then they all hunt for new leaves to race down the stream. "Dodge the riffle!" one of them warns, "Mine got stuck there on the rocks." Another boy uses a long stick to dislodge his own stuck leaf which had stalled out in a pool at a bend in the stream.

Further down the creek, a girl clambers up a leaning tree trunk. She is watching a trio of students who perch on a high bank, enthusiastically poking at a pocket of scum on the water below them. "I know it's not algae," one confidently asserts, "I have a fish tank and when it gets algae it doesn't look anything like this." "Yeah, but I think it IS algae – it's greenish." The third student says, "No ... I think it's pollution. It's gross. It's got bubbles. And when I poke it, it comes apart and then goes together again – I've never seen algae do that..."

Who are these happy hypothesizers? Who are these leaf-racing experts? They are the sixth-grade students, busy at their field work on this Tuesday morning. An hour ago, they got off the bus in a parking lot for the Reston Association. Now they are ready to conduct their usual monthly water quality tests to discover and track the nitrogen, phosphate, dissolved oxygen, pH and temperature of their assigned stream. They compile and record this data before sharing it with the Reston Association's environmental scientists. But while they patiently wait for the chemical indicators to work their wonder in the test tubes, they do what any kid ought to have time to do: they play in the woods!

Later, their play yields academic fruit. When I ask, "How fast did the winning leaf go?" I see them pause to mentally process. One student moves his hand slowly through the air, saying, "It went about this fast." Another says, "Maybe like 15 inches per second," while his classmate recalls, "Wait! That's 'rate' like Ms. Reiter taught us in math this morning!" Her eyes take on an eager intensity as she suddenly makes the connection between "school" and "life." On another day, I will ask the students to brainstorm ways in which they could accurately measure the speed of their leaves. We will verbally weigh the merits of each idea and choose a few to test. But today, I am thrilled to see their ability to translate a concept from an abstraction to its application – excellent progress!

While we snack by the stream, I ask, "Any ideas on how we could figure out what that scummy stuff is?" The students munch on apples and pretzels while giving this thought. "Maybe we could look it up on the internet," one ventures. "Sure," I answer, "so what could we type in the search engine?" They chew thoughtfully. "'Scum'," says one. "Or maybe 'algae' in case it really is algae," another offers. "OK – that's one thing we could try. Any other ideas?" "We could do chemical tests on it!" someone suggests. I nod – they are generating some good strategies for exploring this perplexity! "That definitely would tell us something about whatever it is. What if we collect some of it and look at it under the microscope when we get back to class?" Yes, they like that idea.

When we're done with our snack, Ms. Reiter divides us into our study groups. Green Team goes with Mrs. Balch, Red Team goes with Mrs. P., Yellows go with Ms. Reiter and the Blues go with me. We have already discussed a text which compares and contrasts the characteristics of various maple species. We have decided which components are the likeliest to help us successful identify a "red maple," but this has not been an easy task! Each group has had to wrestle with the vast amount of information given in the article; each group has had to collaboratively determine four characteristics from the ten or twelve listed which should be conclusive, if we do find what we think might be a "red maple." Armed with digital cameras to "prove" their findings, they go a-hunting. There's a maple tree! Can we figure out if it's really a "red"??

When all the detective work is done, the groups reassemble. Mrs. P. asks the students to list the qualities found in scientific observations. She asks them to spend some time writing this type of observation in their science journals. Every student is quickly engrossed in noticing the things surrounding them: trees, flowers, insects, fungus, the sounds, the smells, the textures. They are carefully avoiding any figurative language: no personification, no hyperbole, no metaphor – not yet! But soon, they shift gears. Mrs. P. says, "Now – take one thing you have written about. Put on the perspective of a poet and spend some time writing figuratively about that thing. Write phrases that help us experience what you experience as you listen, breathe, think, feel, and immerse yourself in this setting."

Is this *normal?* Is it normal to see a group of middle school students intently writing poetry by the side of a stream? Normal, yes! Perhaps not "usual," but certainly "normal." God made these children scientists, tree-climbers, team members, poets. He made them inquisitive, active explorers. All we have to do is give them time, space, tools and some guidance. All we have to do is cooperate with God's design. The result is deeply satisfying, to the children and to any who see them so keenly engaged with God's beautiful world.

What makes this vision of learning so rare?

2 MULTIPLE INTELLIGENCES SPOTTED LAST WEEK!

The class has been studying angles. When I ask them to use any method they like to show me what they know about angles, this is what I see:

- One child takes out a ruler and draws several examples, labeling each with its appropriate name: acute, right or square, obtuse.
- Two children decide to lie down on the floor with their feet touching, their arms outstretched, and their straight bodies forming a lovely angle. "90 degrees!" they shout in glee.
- Another student is busy writing a description into her Narration Station notebook. It reads: An angle is formed whenever two lines, rays, or line segments meet…"
- Yet another child stands at my desk, ready to chat. "Well, if it's a skinny one you call it 'acute' just like 'a cute little angle.' But if it's fat, it's like that word for too fat – what is it? Oh yeah, obese – so, the angle is like that only you call it 'obtuse.' The ones that are like the corners of things are square angles, or you *could* call them 'right angles.' It means the same thing."
- Over at a table, one boy is poring over a book of Picasso prints. He is pointing out the angles. "There's a right angle. There's another right angle. Mostly it looks like he used right angles in this one. Oh, wait! There's an… acute angle!"
- "Mrs. Imbody, I need some pipe cleaners." I give the child some pipe cleaners. He twists two of them

together and says, "Pretend the ends are just touching each other and not all bunched up where I twisted them.

- Okay – here's an angle that's probably about 45 degrees 'cause it's half of a right angle." He spreads the pipe cleaners apart a bit. "That's pretty close to 90 degrees, a right angle." He pulls them further apart. "Well, that's really obtuse. It's actually almost 180 degrees, like a straight line."

What's going on here? According to Dr. Howard Gardner, psychologist at Harvard University, I am seeing "Multiple Intelligences" in action. Gardner is credited with devising this theory which identifies types of intelligence ranging from the ones usually measured in IQ tests, "linguistic" and "logical/mathematical," to those labeled "artistic," "spatial," "kinesthetic," and "interpersonal" among others. His theory is now widely accepted in educational psychology circles but is not widely implemented in school settings.

When I once heard Dr. Gardner lecturing on this and other topics, I realized how well-suited Redemptive Education is for recognizing and utilizing these God-given differences in students. When Mrs. Smith asks her kindergarteners to act out the part of *A Midsummer Night's Dream* which they have just listened to, she is utilizing "multiple intelligences." When Mr. Daniels' first-grade class sings rhyming words, they are making the most of "musical" intelligence. Students attempting to write and perform original puppet shows are reliant on linguistic, artistic, interpersonal, spatial and kinesthetic intelligences. We can instruct *and* assess our students with Multiple Intelligences in mind.

Our amazing Creator demonstrates, not surprisingly, an amazing creativity in the unique combination of talents, learning styles, physical traits and character qualities He has placed within each individual. Redemptive Educators value and appreciate those unique combinations. Furthermore, they seek to nurture the development of each child, by employing those intelligences natural to the child, and also by introducing those that are less familiar to the child.

3 THINK-SAY-DO PART ONE: *THINK*

"Let the words of my mouth and the meditations of my heart
be acceptable to You, O Lord, my Rock and my Redeemer!
Let everything I say —
Let everything I do —
Let everything I think and choose
reflect Your grace and truth!" (song by AEI)

Our lives as human beings consist largely of what we think, what we say, and what we do. Our *value* does not consist in these things; our *value* is entirely based on God's love for us. "Not that we loved Him, but that He loved us ..." (I John 4:10).

But as moral agents, as people created in the image of God, our choices lie in the regions of what we cultivate in our "interior" — that is, our spirit, soul, and mind; what we choose to say; and what we choose to do.

God's word gives us a perfect starting point in Philippians 4:19, with its exhortation to "think on these things": all that is **T**rue, **H**onorable, **R**ight, **P**ure, **L**ovely, of **G**ood repute, **E**xcellent, and **W**orthy of praise. Students snap their fingers and sing the silly **THRPLGEW** song to help them remember to think on these things! Music is a powerful entry point to our minds and hearts. It provides a swift, smooth pathway to fueling our "meditations." It follows that cultivating in our children a love and appreciation for beautiful music in a variety of genres, with melody, harmony and lyric that convey truth and grace, whether by "sound" or by text, is a natural way to edify their interior person. It also follows that ugly, meaningless, vapid and false "sound" and text are detrimental to the development of our beautiful children.

Psalm 139 affirms, "Thou dost understand my thought from afar" (verse 2). God knows each thought! He does not hold us accountable for those gypsy thoughts that arrive unwelcome at the doorstep of our mind: He does encourage us that He understands these thoughts: He does exhort us to "take every thought captive to Christ" (II Corinthians 10:5). We can't choose who shows up, but we can choose whom we will entertain! We can help our children know that they need not fear their own thoughts - that there is a Shepherd who can tame even these wild things, and that one strategy for taking thoughts captive is to so fill one's mind with THRPLGEW that there is hardly room for the renegades.

Most of us rightly understand that how we think about ourselves is significant. Contemporary cultural consensus, however, is "off" when it states the importance of our having a high self-esteem, and the dangers of our having a low self-esteem. According to Tim Keller, in his slim book entitled *The Freedom of Self-Forgetfulness,* contemporary cultural consensus runs counter to history and even counter to other cultures' thinking in its appraisal of self-esteem. Where current popular opinion generally attributes bad behavior and character to low self-esteem, most people in most times and most places have concluded that bad behavior and character are the result of *hubris,* an over-inflated view of oneself! Keller contends that the proper way to think about one's identity is not to let it be defined either by others' opinions of us, nor even of our own opinion of ourselves, but rather by God's opinion of us. His word is rich with truth and grace with which to discover who we really are, and where our value and identity lie.

An ancient prayer invites God to "cleanse the thoughts of our hearts by the inspiration of Thy Holy Spirit" – a washing, a purifying for which each one of us thirsts and which brings, though perhaps logically inexplicable, an experience of the Lord's healing, correcting, restorative ministry into the deepest parts of ourselves.

4 THINK-SAY-DO PART 2: *SAY*

"From the abundance of the heart the mouth speaks." Matthew 12:34

The morning comes, and with it Thy new mercies,
Thy faithfulness with every dawning day,
and we rejoice to seek Thy holy purpose
in all we think, in all we do, in all we say! (song by AEI)

Our interior – heart, mind, imagination, soul, spirit – is the source of our speech. Internal realities shape external things that become evident to others: what we say and what we do. Speech and action are the means by which we respond to and communicate with God, people, and the created world. Our Maker understands our thought from afar (Ps 139:2) but everyone else must figure it out by listening to our words and observing our actions.

   Part of classical study includes a high regard for literature that has been found to be of enduring value, that addresses universal human issues and interests by means of language demonstrating beauty, elegance, insight and skill. Drawing upon the best poetry, story, argument and exposition that human culture has produced provides excellent "food" for our children's souls. In reading and listening to that excellent "food" – receiving it – digesting it – analyzing it – meditating on it – responding to it – our children profit from the thoughts of people far removed from their parochial experience. Memorizing this language, reciting this language, both individually and as a group, creates a confluence of our own and others' ideas and words. It is as if the stream of our thinking and discourse becomes enlivened, oxygenated in its white-water tumble over classical literature.

This is why we can invite even our youngest children to sing, "Let the words of my mouth and the meditations of my heart be acceptable in Thy sight, O Lord, my Rock and my Redeemer!" This is why we invite students to memorize portions of *The Rime of the Ancient Mariner,* why we join as a whole learning community to recite Psalm 139, why we read aloud in unison the ancient prayers of the church and teach the ancient lyrics from the ancient hymns of the faith.

Even as our thinking shapes our speech, so does our speaking shape our thought. We explicitly model for our children how to make our voices convey respect, how to answer the question, "Can you say that in a more gracious way?" We demonstrate the power of a "leader voice," and practice using whisper voices when appropriate. We value lovely language, rich vocabulary, sophisticated metaphor, and individual student "voice." What we say matters: how we say it matters.

We choose what kinds of words we will use, and what their messages will convey. "I tell you," Jesus exhorts each one of us, "on the day of judgment people will give account for every careless word they speak" (Matthew 12:36). What a mercy it is that we can ask with the psalmist that God "open our lips that our mouths might show forth Thy praise!" (Ps. 51:15). God gives us the potent gift of language, sending us His Son as the Living Word.

Come quickly, Lord, and bring Thy peaceful presence!
Come, Morning Star of never-ending Day,
and we'll rejoice to seek Thy holy purpose
in all we think, in all we do, in all we say! (song by AEI)

5 THINK-SAY-DO PART 3: *DO*

Even a child is known by his actions, by whether his conduct is pure and right.
(Proverbs 20:11)

Thinking – speaking – doing: most of our daily life is comprised of these three. All contribute to each other, and all are worthy of attention. In this third in a trio of essays, we explore the significance of "action" – of "doing" – in teaching and in learning. Research indicates that having children gesture, move purposefully, or physically manipulate something in the course of their learning helps new information to "stick," and to "stick" longer. In other words, involving our bodies in acquisition of data or skills or concepts increases our comprehension AND our retention.

This is why Redemptive Educators build in "legitimate motion" to their lesson plans. Whatever our curriculum, we maximize it when we invite children to be explorers and adventurers, uncovering hidden treasures, rather than passive receptacles of data. Redemptive Educators facilitate experiential learning: opportunities for the children in their classes to touch, hold, manipulate, and interact with the things about which they study.

In a class of sixth graders, the young scientists donned nitrile gloves to carefully examine a tiny Common Yellowthroat whose unfortunate (and fatal) collision with a brick building made it possible for us to bring it into the classroom. Students marveled at its delicate black and yellow feathers, its tiny sharp-clawed perching feet, the under-feathers of its outspread wing. They measured the wingspan, consulted the birdsong books to hear what its song would have been (*"whichety-whichety"*), researched its diet, nesting patterns, and habitat. Their "doing" led to a new level of "knowing." They sketched, they wrote description – but mostly they "experienced" this tiny creature and understood in a new way the claim by its Creator that He knows even when one little bird falls.

From all of this "doing" there developed "loving." How carefully they cradled the body of the bird! Gentle fingers stroked the smooth breast feathers. The scientists forgot themselves completely in engaging with this bird. How fervently they exclaimed on its beauty and intricacy – without any necessity for prompting on my part. Eagerly they asked if their teacher could help them dissect the bird to further discover its design. What a different experience altogether than merely having been assigned the reading of a paragraph in a textbook on the topic of "birds."

When we teach our children to honor others, we know that words are one part of that "honoring," but the expression on our faces and the sound of our voices are also important components! Wise parents and teachers explicitly model and provide practice for a "friendly look" or a "respectful countenance." We teach our young scholars to tuck in their shirts and enter the Sanctuary with dignity. When we stand to sing a hymn, or to pledge allegiance to the flag, we demonstrate an erect stance, with shoulders back and eyes alert. These are not a substitute for heart attitudes, but they can cultivate those attitudes which ultimately bless the child, the surrounding community, and God.

Corrie Ten Boom, a dear saint of the Lord who was imprisoned by the Nazis during WWII for her family's protection of persecuted Jews, recounts her experience of God's miraculous transformational power. After her release, and after the war, as she travelled the world speaking of God's forgiveness and grace in the darkest places, Corrie saw a person in the audience whom she instantly recognized as one of the former prison guards. This guard had been merciless and cruel – but now, with a glowing face and an outstretched hand, he was approaching her to share that he, too, had become a believer in Christ! Corrie describes the nanoseconds of WWIII within in her heart. *How* could she possibly forgive this man? *How* could she possibly shake his hand? In pure obedience to Christ – with no sense of love whatsoever – Corrie reached out her own trembling hand to grasp his: and in that *action*, God's Spirit poured into her spirit an overwhelming and miraculous change of heart: she *loved* this man!

Sometimes, love will call us to action. Sometimes, knowing will compel us to doing. But it is also true that action can lead to both knowing and loving. A Biblical understanding of the goal of education comprises all three: knowing – loving – doing, each fueling the others, each leading to growth in the others, all choreographing a dance of delight in God, His creation, and His people.

Scriptures that may serve as meditation on this topic include:

*But prove yourselves **doers** of the word, and not merely hearers who delude themselves... He who looks into the perfect law of liberty and continues in it, and is not a forgetful hearer but a **doer** of the work, this one will be blessed in what he **does**. (James 1:25)*

*The things you have learned and received and heard and seen in me, **practice** these things (Philippians 4:9)*

*Therefore, gird your minds for **action** ... (I Peter 1:13)*

*Whatever your hand finds to **do, do** it with all your might! (Ecclesiastes 9:10)*

*A good understanding have all they who **do** Thy commands. (Psalm. 111:10)*

6 QUALITY PRODUCERS

Poppleton the Pig, that venerable hero of Cynthia Rylant's picture
books, spends a night camping in a tent. The story reports that
"sometimes he was reading, sometimes he was thinking, sometimes
he was just paying attention." Luckily for him, he was not a student at
an Aurora, IL middle school, whose motto on the sign outside their
building reads: "Educating Students to be Quality Producers."
Although Poppleton enjoys the chirping of the crickets and the other
musical sounds of the summer night (which he notices by "paying
attention"), it appears that he subsequently fails to "produce"
anything which might justify such a use of his time. What a waste.

For some season of his life (including his years in school),
Albert Einstein, like Poppleton, spent many hours reading, thinking,
and paying attention (although not to the lectures in his classes.)
After his "education," he settled for a low-level position at the
counter of the patent office, where, for the next seven years, he read,
thought, doodled on paper, and paid attention to something in his
mind. Then, you might say, he became a "quality producer." He
produced "$E=mc^2$" – not bad for a do-nothing kind of a guy.

Evangelical philosopher Robert C. Roberts (Distinguished
Professor of Ethics, Baylor University) describes his own early
endeavors in this way: "I was a busy child, mostly with business of
my own making, most of which was nonintellectual. ... I tried to sell
garden produce to the local grocery store... Dad built scooters and
go-carts and I worked at it with him, but I never became much good
at things mechanical... I hunted and fished... I practiced the guitar a
lot..." Apparently, he wasn't winning any "Most Likely to Succeed in
Philosophy" awards.

The word "producer" works best in the context of biology,
economics, or industry. It is not a word for boys and girls, nor for

those who educate them. Our business is helping children explore God's world and discover their place in it. We cannot measure our success in this endeavor with standardized test scores (although they are useful in a limited sort of way), nor by percentages of words spelled correctly on a quiz (although they may tell us how better to teach spelling), nor by any overzealous attempt to evaluate the hearts, minds and spirits of our children. We are daily dealing with the hidden things of the soul – desires, thoughts, ideas, and wills. We want to *equip* students to follow God's high calling in their lives; we just don't know yet exactly what those callings may be! So, we are careful to teach every child to the best of our abilities, so that they may have capable tools at the ready: reading, writing, estimating, calculating, imagining, discussing, analyzing, serving.

Gardeners know that at a certain time of year, some plants spring up overnight, verdant and vibrant, while many others still crouch under the moist earth, waiting. They're filling up, they're developing, and at the right time, they too will poke themselves up out of the mulch and into the sunshine. Of those plants, some are certainly "quality producers," (beans, for example), while many others produce nothing at all, except, perhaps, sweet fragrance, bright color, or a cooling shade.

Let's *not* educate students to be "quality producers." What a countercultural idea! We will need to help one another remember that "production" is not the goal. Instead, let's pray that our work in our children's lives will bear much fruit – quality fruit! – fragrant, colorful, wonderful fruit created in them by Christ Jesus.

7 WHO ARE THEY?

They are young children. They are wearing plaid jumpers and white blouses, polo shirts and navy shorts. They are entering the school on a weekday morning. Who are they?

Our students, of course! But what does that mean? If we reflect for just a moment on the fact that they are people, created in the image of God, and if we reflect for just a moment more, considering who that God is, and what He is like, we will realize several things about these children.

They are spiritual beings: They worship! They were created to worship! The essential part of them is much more than what we see, much more than the sum of their appearance, speech, behavior, and intellect.

They are creative beings: They invent! They are designed to take initiative, to devise, and to make things. They were born with minds that have ideas, that search and strategize, that motivate them to act upon their environments.

They are social beings: They interact! They need time with others, as well as time alone. Families, friends, and the body of Christ are their necessary companions. They have a part to play in relationships with others, with the world, and with God. They are members of neighborhoods, cultures and countries. Their gifts are essential to the rest of us. Laughing, hugging, smiling and touching are mandatory components in their lives.

They are rational beings: They think! They need abundant nutritious food for their minds as much as they need it for their bodies. We can expect them to consider data and draw conclusions. We can expect that they have ways of learning and ways of knowing, whether or not they articulate them. Educators and parents serve children well when they help them understand interrelationships, connections that make up an integral reality, not a fragmented jumble of unrelated facts.

They are aesthetic beings: They admire! The best of books, music, and art are not wasted on children. Their classroom environment, the quality of their materials – these details matter if you are working with aesthetic beings. Beautiful words, beautifully spoken – this is how to learn poetry and scripture! Clear unison, close harmony – children can learn to sing this way!

They are responsible beings: They conduct themselves! "Even a child is known by his actions" and even small children are able to increasingly grow in responsibility for who they are. "Let no one look down on your youth" – we know that children are capable of changing the world! We expect them to be developing into people who look at needs, and think, "How can I help?"

They are physical beings: They move! Running, dancing, waving arms, shouting, hopping, crawling on all fours: these are appropriate actions for physical beings! Learning *when* to run, dance, wave arms, shout, hop, or crawl on all fours is the tricky part, and it doesn't happen overnight. Students are asked to be focused, still and quiet for short periods of time, then given directions for "legitimate motion" before they become too restless. Recess is not used as a reward but as the necessary free-play time that healthy children require. Active learning is encouraged as students dance out the water cycle, or stomp and gallop to Copland's "Rodeo." Time to eat and time to rest, time to work and time to play are all equally important for physical beings. And although these present bodies grow old and break down, we have the promise of resurrection life which will raise them up once again, never to grow old!

Wow - These are complex people! They cannot be reduced to any single part of themselves. Every aspect was created by God. Every aspect matters. Everything we do in school should minister to the whole person: body, soul and spirit. That's what's behind our use of curriculum that features games and manipulatives. That's why we teach using "integral curriculum" with its focus on connections and "the whole picture." That's why we need every part of the school community to help, to serve, to pray and to advise as we plan and implement each year's themes.

8 HOLY UNSAMENESS

In his book, *The Cube and the Cathedral*, author George Weigel describes two architectural landmarks in Paris. One is La Grande Arche de la Défense - a stark immensity, perfectly symmetrical, whose gleaming marble sides are filled with the offices of the International Foundation for Human Rights. It is a veritable monument to atheistic humanism. Guide books explain that the entire Notre Dame Cathedral – towers, spires and all - could fit within the vast, empty interior of La Grande Arche.

The other landmark structure is the Notre Dame Cathedral itself. The author asks, "Which culture... would better protect human rights? Which culture would more firmly secure the moral foundations of democracy? The culture that built this stunning, rational, angular, geometrically precise but *essentially featureless* cube? Or the culture that produced the vaulting and bosses, the gargoyles and flying buttresses, the nooks and crannies, the *asymmetries and holy 'unsameness'* of Notre-Dame and the other great Gothic cathedrals of Europe?"

While Weigel deals primarily with questions of culture, politics, and religion, his contrast of the "essentially featureless cube" and the "asymmetries and holy 'unsameness'" of the cathedral prompts me to think about our interest in nurturing the uniqueness of each child." Examining every word in this phrase proves to be an illuminating exercise!

- "nurturing" – feeding, cultivating, educating, protecting from harm.
- "uniqueness" – the quality of being one-of-a-kind.
- "each" – specifically individual, separate.
- "child" – the still-developing, immature human being.

It is undeniably convenient to deal with cubes. You can stack them, pack them, count them swiftly by rows and columns, and accurately measure both their perimeters and their volumes. They do not do unexpected things. If you've worked with one cube, you know the essential qualities of any cube. How efficient! A cube-producing place does not have to be complicated.

But when we begin not only to *deal with* but actually to *nurture* "the nooks and crannies," "the gargoyles and flying buttresses," "the asymmetries and holy 'unsameness'" found in the human child (soul, body, and spirit) we have a complex and delicate task. It is not convenient. You cannot stack them, pack them, or even count them swiftly, as we have discovered. You cannot even imagine the extent of their perimeters nor can you measure their infinite interiors. They constantly do unexpected things. No matter how many children you have worked with, there is always some new surprise. It is not an efficient proposition. It is a sacred calling: a vocation.

Look at a child: do you see nooks and crannies? A few gargoyles here and there? What about asymmetries? Can we bear it? What do we do about those flying buttresses, anyway? Can we learn to delight in the "holy unsameness" that so delighted our God as He created poets and accountants, judges and janitors, dancers and mechanics and all that untidy jumble of little children?

One of the reasons Redemptive Educators love multi-age classes is that we can capitalize on the "holy unsameness" of the children. Students are stimulated, comforted, challenged and blessed by working with others who are older, younger, quieter, sillier, cleverer, gentler or better at math. They learn appreciation for the myriad gifts represented in their classmates: they learn humility and patience with their own faults, and those of others. They become the big sisters, little brothers, neighbors and friends that make our school a community.

Every once in a while, we get poked by someone's "spire" or taken aback by a "gargoyle." We get lost in someone's "vaulting" and are baffled by his "bosses." Those are the times to practice patience, good humor, and humility in the face of deep mysteries. Those are the times to praise Him for the uniqueness of each child. As Gerard Manley Hopkins says in his poem, "Pied Beauty":

GLORY be to God for dappled things,
For skies of couple-color as a brinded cow,
For rose-moles all in stipple upon trout that swim;
Fresh-firecoal chestnut-falls, finches' wings;
Landscape plotted and pieced, fold, fallow and plough,
And all trades, their gear and tackle and trim.
All things counter, original, spare, strange,
Whatever is fickle, freckled (who knows how?)
With swift, slow; sweet, sour; adazzle, dim.
He fathers-forth whose beauty is past change;
Praise him.

9 OF CENTIPEDES AND CORN SEEDS

Jared hoists a rock from its bed in the forest floor. "Look, guys! Centipedes!" His buddies come running to see. "Those are millipedes." "No, they're not! They're centipedes!" "How do you know?" "They have more legs!" "No, they don't!" "Get the book – quick, before they get away!" One boy retrieves a well-worn volume from the field backpack. He flips through pages, muttering, "Centipedes, centipedes…" The other boy urges, "Look in the back! Look in the back! In the index!" Then a triumphant yell, "They ARE centipedes!!" "How can you tell?" "Don't touch them! They can bite!" "But millipedes aren't poisonous!" "I know, but centipedes are! Look, these guys only have *one* pair of legs for each body segment – plus, look at those long whiskers – that is *definitely* a centipede!" "Let's catch one and take it back to the room!" "Well, then we have to catch something for it to eat, too! Look for a worm or a spider..." and off they go to search for a meal for their new classroom pet. That week, Jared et al. make an informational video featuring "Legs" (as the centipede has been christened) and take turns posing faux Jeopardy questions for a classroom game about the differences between centipedes, millipedes, and insects.

Serena brings a retired Indian corn cob to class. Thanksgiving was months ago, and her mother doesn't want it around, since it has been attracting mice to nibble its blue and yellow kernels. Serena shows her it to her teacher. "What would you like us to do with it, Serena?" Ms. Johnson asks. "Can we turn it into cornmeal like the Lakota did?" Serena inquires. "We can try!" says her teacher. "Any other ideas?" "Maybe we could plant some. The Lakota definitely wouldn't waste it by just throwing it away!" Her teacher agrees. Later, the class spends a few hours outdoors, first trying various methods to dislodge the corn from the cob, then using rocks and thick sticks to attempt grinding the stony kernels into cornmeal. "This is *really* hard," Serena reports. "It would take forever to get enough cornmeal for one little piece of cornbread!" She turns her attention to finding a good place in the school garden to try growing the corn instead. She decides to place several kernels in one corner of a raised bed, and a few others in a planting pot in a different spot. Over the next days and weeks, she races outside at the first opportunity to inspect the two plantings. It turns into a competition between "bed" and "pot," with classmates predicting which seeds will sprout first, inspiring more students to bring old Indian corn from their homes, as well. A collaboration develops among the children, who share cornhusks to assemble little huts and figures in a "village" of their own invention. As the corn does or doesn't sprout, the children hypothesize about cause and effect; they adjust variables; they measure to see whose corn is currently the tallest; they predict whether the corn will eventually produce more cobs; they pluck corn worm and Japanese beetles off the stalks. Later, their "free writing" in the classroom is chiefly preoccupied with reporting on the progress of their project, along with fanciful stories set in a tiny cornhusk village.

This is experiential learning! Sure, it's fun – but it's also packed full of educational goodness, with nary a textbook or worksheet in sight. Highly engaged and motivated students are energetically pursuing a deeper understanding of God's world and their place in it. And if we analyze what is really going on in the two above scenarios, we might be surprised to see how much academic, social, physical and even spiritual development is taking place! In fact, pause a moment to look back at each vignette, asking: What school "subjects" are represented? What academic skills are students practicing? What social skills are being honed? What scriptural principles are in play? Take another moment to ask yourself: What is the teacher's role in these "lessons"? What is the children's role? Who is doing the work, and what kind of work is it? What resources of time and materiel are required? What kind of learning is occurring as these children joyfully experience interaction with the natural world God invites them to discover?

Experiential learning, one of the core tenets of Redemptive Education, can (and should) happen within the classroom, of course. But there is an intensity and longevity in the kind of learning children do when they are out "in the field." Why?

The very first lessons humankind encountered were in a garden tailor-made for their education and enjoyment. God infused the entire creation with expressions of His beauty, His power, His character. The world was a panoply of sensory dynamism: color, fragrance, sound; movement of water, wind, and muscle; texture, shape, brightness and shadow. Into this garden Adam and Eve were invited, not only for sensory pleasure, but also for the distinct satisfaction of having been entrusted with good work as God's appointed stewards. Flora and fauna fostered delight, wonder, and the choosing of particular names for each beloved flower and creature. Fresh and fully oxygenated air, fellowship with their Maker, and lots of physical activity combined to create a wholesome robustness to our first parents' bodies, minds and spirits.

It is out in the natural world that their children (and ours!) are most able to thrive and grow. They learn to observe, to explore and to serve with affection the plants, animals, birds and bugs they encounter in the meadow, woods, streams and gardens. Especially in this cultural season of much "sitting around," "staring at screens," or officially "playing sports," our children are often denied the birthright of initiative, contemplation, action, observation and exploration of the world God created for them to love and to know. Mental, physical and spiritual health increase when students have plenty of unstructured time outside. The best teachers will make use of the true "curriculum" that emerges almost effortlessly from children's encounters with nature.

Notice how Jesus says, "Consider the birds" or "Consider the lilies" or "Do you see the fields white for harvest?" He warns about weeds springing up among wheat; and even the wind and the waves obey Him. How can our children profit from His word if they do not know birds, lilies, weeds, wheat, wind, and waves enough to consider them? What if the natural world is too foreign for them to understand His teaching?

Let's get our students out in the woods, in the fields, on the beach, in the snow, in the sun, in the wind, in the rain. It is their birthright, and our powerful ally in Christ-centered Redemptive Education. Allow them to handle, discover, observe, and minister to the ladybugs, lizards, sassafras and snakes. Our children can (and will) acquire skills in math, science, reading, writing, teamwork, independence and everything else with more real rigor and energy when they emerge from the context of engagement in God's astonishing and wonderful world – experiential learning!

10 TO TELL A STORY

In his memoir, *Where the Wind Leads,* Dr. Vinh Chung, who as a tiny boy escaped with his large family as Vietnamese refugees known as "boat people," describes his mother's approach to disciplining her ten children. "She never shouted or got angry; she just told us stories that always had a moral or lesson attached... Some stories were tragic, and some were inspiring, and she had a way of telling them in a calm and quiet voice that could reduce us to tears" (pp. 279-80).

Jesus also used stories in surprising and powerful ways. Like Vinh's mother, sometimes he told a story instead of giving an expected response to someone's action or inquiry. Observing the peoples' propensity for picking the places of honor at a dinner he attended, Jesus told a story (Luke 14:16-24). When the Pharisees began to grumble, saying, "This man receives sinners and eats with them," Jesus delivered a trio of tales featuring a sheep, a coin, and a prodigal son (Luke 15:4-32). When somebody was bothered about his sibling's unfair division of the family inheritance, Jesus told him a story about a rich man who had laid up treasures for himself, but was not "rich toward God" (Luke 12:16-21).

Leo Widrich explains some of the science behind the power of story from a December 2012 posting at www.lifehacker.com:

> We all enjoy a good story, whether it's a novel, a movie, or simply something one of our friends is explaining to us. But why do we feel so much more engaged when we hear a narrative about events?
>
> It's in fact quite simple. If we listen to a powerpoint presentation with boring bullet points, a certain part in the brain gets activated. Scientists call

this Broca's area and Wernicke's area. Overall, it hits our language processing parts in the brain, where we decode words into meaning. And that's it, nothing else happens.

When we are being told a story, things change dramatically. Not only are the language processing parts in our brain activated, but any other area in our brain that we would use when experiencing the events of the story are too.

If someone tells us about how delicious certain foods were, our sensory cortex lights up. If it's about motion, our motor cortex gets active...

Widrich describes a study in which subjects' brains were monitored as they encountered sensory-rich figurative language:

Metaphors like 'The singer had a velvet voice' and 'He had leathery hands' roused the sensory cortex. [...] Then, the brains of participants were scanned as they read sentences like "John grasped the object" and "Pablo kicked the ball." The scans revealed activity in the motor cortex, which coordinates the body's movements...

Widrich concludes: "A story can put your whole brain to work."

The Creator God designed our minds for story. Widrich asserts, "We are wired that way," although he attributes this to evolutionary engineering rather than to any divine purpose or plan. He continues his explanation:

A story, if broken down into the simplest form, is a connection of cause and effect. And that is exactly how we think. We think in narratives all day long, no matter if it is about buying groceries, whether we think about work or our spouse at home. We make up (short) stories in our heads for every action and conversation.

... whenever we hear a story, we want to relate it to one of our existing experiences. That's why metaphors work so well with us. While we are busy searching for a similar experience in our brains, we activate a part called insula, which helps us relate to that same experience of pain, joy, or disgust.

Is it any wonder that Redemptive Educators find "story" so compelling a strategy for teaching our children? As parents, we might explore how to maximize use of this powerful approach whenever we instruct, comfort, correct, discipline, encourage or exhort our young disciples.

11 THE BEST BOOKS

"The best thought the world possesses is stored in books;
we must open books to children, the best books!"
Charlotte Mason

Have you ever heard a parent say, "Oh, I don't mind if Susie, my first grader, only eats gummy bears. I am just glad she's eating *something!* We love to take her to the grocery store every week so she can stock up on gummies ...'? And you've probably never encountered a parent who says, "We're so thrilled that Johnny drinks Coke all day! You know it's so important for children to stay hydrated! We order cases of Coke to be delivered to our door."

But perhaps you *have* heard parents say, "Well, I know that the *Captain Underpants* series is inane at best, but we're just so glad that our child is reading *something!*" Maybe you've said something like that yourself! It is understandable that when our previously resistant seven-year-old is found with his nose buried in a book, laughing out loud at every page turn, we are likely to feel a great sense of relief that *at last* he is choosing to read.

There are lots of us out there. Today I saw this book review, written by a parent whose child is going gaga over *The Diary of a Wimpy Kid* series: "Any book that can get my non-reader interested in reading is fantastic with me!" Another like-minded parent wrote, "I'm thrilled for my son to be wanting to read anything, so I don't censor these titles, but I don't think [Greg Heffley, the main character] is a good role model."

We can hope that the latter was meant to be an understatement. After all, this character is a boy whose discourse routinely includes references to "jerks," "hot girls," "cute butts," and worse. His daily activities feature lying to parents, shirking responsibilities, bullying others, and worse. As if these were not objectionable enough, the above are all portrayed as being "funny" – and the children do laugh, believe me. The vulnerable young readers who comprise the *Wimpy Kid* fan club are led into sympathetic identification with the character and his base habits.

Before we are too hard on Jeff Kinney, the wildly successful author of the *Wimpy* series, consider that he evidently thought he was writing a book for adults. *The Telegraph* online quotes Kinney: "I meant for my book to be read by grown-ups. I thought I was writing a book that was, at most, a look back on childhood by an adult. I worked on it for eight years and then my publisher told me I had written a book for children." (Shame on the publisher!)

Why do we expect our children just to "know" it *isn't* humorous to deceive others, to speak with disrespect to a teacher, to think of people in terms of their anatomy, or to pursue selfishness at cost to our neighbors? Why do we think our child's understanding is mature and nuanced enough to "know" that even though we supply her with books whose characters are named "Professor Poopy Pants" and similar, we don't actually approve? Unless you would like your second-grader to emulate the "humor" she reads in a story, you'd better not signal your tacit approval by putting that story in her hands.

A robust body of research tells us that even adults are highly influenced in our behavior, language, and attitudes by what we've read. According to a study published in the March 2012 issue of *British Social Psychology*, adult readers reflected increased levels of both physical and relational aggression after reading stories in which the characters demonstrated these aggressions. Evidently, "provoked people who were given the opportunity to engage in a specific form of retaliatory violence were more likely to do so if they had just read a fictional account of similar activity."

In another 2012 study we learn that, "readers who identify with fictional characters are prone to subconsciously adopt their behavior ... bookworms have been shown to adopt the feelings, thoughts, beliefs and internal responses of fictional characters they relate to in a phenomenon called 'experience-taking'." You can see the problem when young children are invited to identify with a character whose "feelings, thoughts, beliefs and internal responses" as well as language and actions are completely contrary to all that is "true, honorable, right, pure, lovely, of good repute, excellent and worthy of praise" (Philippians 4:8).

The good news is that children, like adults, can be influenced *positively* when immersed in a book featuring beautiful language, rich imagery, and a quest for high ideals. A story's main character does not have to be cloyingly sweet or unwaveringly noble, however. Three dimensional, authentic characters can contribute to the shaping of our children's hearts, minds, and motives. As our boys and girls read great books, they join the adventures of literary companions who are living out the struggles common to us all, while attaining a morally satisfying level of growth and development.

So: bring on the books! But let's do our best to make sure these are "living books," as 19th century educational reformer Charlotte Mason would call them. After all, as she cautions us, "That children like feeble and tedious story books, does not at all prove that these are wholesome food; they like lollipops but cannot live upon them!" Let's give them tales that can nourish their souls, "the best books" – yes!

12 SO WHAT SHOULD THEY READ?

It's all very well to castigate *Captain Underpants* and denounce *The Diary of a Wimpy Kid*. But if we aren't going to give our young readers these banal books, and if they do prefer the "silly," the "playful" and the "funny," what should they read?

For very young readers, the slim chapter books featuring Mr. Putter and his cat, Tabby, are excellent in the "edifying but funny" department. In this extensive series, we can join the title characters as they "Run the Race," "Toot the Horn," and "Take the Train," (although I would be remiss if I did not warn you that the latter involves subterfuge ☺). Along the same lines are the Allan Ahlberg "Gaskitts Adventures" such as *The Cat Who Got Carried Away*, which cleverly incorporate maps, timelines and visually hilarious supporting illustrations.

In the "silly" department we can also find a trio of tales from Doreen Cronin featuring the fearless watchdog, J. J. Tully, and his posse of chickens. *The Trouble with Chickens, The Legend of Diamond Lil*, and *The Chicken Squad* invite early chapter book readers into harmless and humorous misadventures with a retired search-and-rescue dog and some frisky chicks.

Kate DeCamillo, the National Ambassador for Young People's Literature and author of two Newbery Medal winners, introduces children to a diminutive cowboy and his horse, Maybelline, in *Leroy Ninker Saddles Up*. DeCamillo serves up rich vocabulary via whimsical dialogue between Leroy and Maybelline's original owner, who notices that Mr. Ninker "looks to be in need of assistance with some of life's more overwhelming necessities." She exhorts him to "listen to the people of the world when they give you informational bits" and to be "a straightforward communicator." Excellent counsel for all of us!

Of course, there are the "oldies but goodies." Beverly Cleary's stories, many set in the fifties and sixties of my childhood, have characters like Henry Huggins, his dog Ribsy, and the neighborhood pest, Ramona. Their timeless antics, adventures and mishaps unfold in the context of loving families and friendly communities.

For those who delight in whimsy, try the whole series by Betty MacDonald featuring *Mrs. Piggle-Wiggle* and her mysterious, magical cures such as "The Never-Want-To-Go-To-Bedders-Cure" or "The Won't-Pick-Up-Toys-Cure" (hmm... we might like to consult Mrs. Piggle-Wiggle ourselves...!) Anyone who lives in an upside-down house and was married to a pirate once upon a time is sure to be an interesting character. ("Mrs. Piggle-Wiggle says that when she was a little girl she used to lie in bed and gaze up at the ceiling and wonder and wonder what it would be like if the house were upside down. And so, when she grew up and built her own house, she had it built upside down, just to see ..." Now – didn't you wonder and wonder about that very thing when you were a child? I did!)

For a similar sort of old-fashioned "silly," we cannot do better than the real, original *Winnie-the-Pooh* by A. A. Milne. If you want wisdom along with your whimsy, then hearken to this Bear of Little Brain who somehow effectively explains the ephemeral: "Well," said Pooh, "what I like best," and then he had to stop and think. Because although Eating Honey was a very good thing to do, there was a moment just before you began to eat it which was better than when you were, but he didn't know what it was called."

Whatever it's called, there is a delicious moment "just before" we pick up a new book and open its cover. And then: let the story begin! Whether silly, or serious, funny or philosophical: invite your children to "feast" on the best books!

13 THE THINGS REVEALED

"The secret things belong to the Lord our God, but the things revealed belong to us and to our children forever!" (Deuteronomy 29:29)

Imagine a large poster of an iceberg in frigid arctic waters. A small portion of the iceberg is above the surface of the water, gleaming white. Most of the iceberg is submerged in the blue ocean, revealed to us only by the eye of the photographer. From this visual metaphor, we get the phrase "the tip of the iceberg" and understand this to mean that what we can perceive is a fraction of the whole, merely a hint at what lies beneath the surface, hidden from our view.

The iceberg serves as visual metaphor for the verse above, as well. All that is mysterious, all that is unknown, all that is perplexing, all that is bewildering – these "secret things" belong to the Lord our God, who knows them wholly and who sees them clearly from before "the beginning" to beyond "the end." From all the infinite realm of "things to be known," the human race has been given only a portion – the vast remainder are, as yet, "the secret things."

But God invites us to explore! And so, we invite our children to explore God's world and discover their place in it with us as their joyful co-adventurers in the journey! "The things revealed belong to us and to our children forever" – and these "things revealed" are bountiful enough to keep us busy for quite a long while, it would seem.

How do we see "the things revealed"? How do we explore and discover?

God reveals Himself to us through His creation – through the natural world. "For His invisible attributes, namely, His eternal power and divine nature, have been clearly perceived, ever since the creation of the world, in the things that have been made." (Romans 1:19-20) For this reason we spend a lot of time outside: watching, listening, playing, drawing, describing, noticing, admiring, enjoying God's creation.

God reveals Himself to us through His word as found in the Bible. He exhorts parents and teachers to equip their children with deep knowledge of His principles, His truth, His commandments. "When you walk about, they will guide you; when you sleep, they will guard you; and when you awake, they will talk with you. For the commandment is a lamp and the teaching is a light." (Proverbs 6:22-23) For this reason we help our children and ourselves to pay attention to God's word. We read it, hear it, memorize and sing it, and find in it "everything pertaining to life and godliness, through the true knowledge of Him who called us by His own glory and excellence." (2 Peter 1:3)

Finally, and most intimately, God reveals Himself to us through our relationship with Him: Father, Son, and Holy Spirit. He says, "I will instruct you and teach you in the way you should go: I will guide you with My eye." (Psalm 32:8) But how can God guide us with His eye? Have you ever given a significant glance towards your husband or wife, your child or your friend? A glance that says, "Look at THAT!" or "Don't do that," or "Let's get out of here!" Your husband, your wife, your child and your friend know that "look" because they know *you!* They understand your thoughts and feelings because of a long history of communication with you – when they see your "look," they know exactly what you are thinking, what you are "saying."

I like to spend time on a porch on a mountain, writing and reading and looking into the mysterious woods below the house. If I want to see the secretive wild creatures who live in that wood, my best strategy is to watch my cat, Jericho, who sleeps on my lap as I sit on the porch. When Jericho looks, I look: and there is the fox! the deer! the bear with her cubs! Wherever my cat directs his attention, I direct my attention and discover – revealed! – the things that had formerly been concealed, "the secret things."

For this reason, we prayerfully work to cultivate our own and our children's relationship with the Lord our God, and with one another as His children. We invite all to explore God's world and discover their place in it. This is our mission! This is our privilege. "The things revealed belong to us and to our children forever!"

14 "SAVORY FOOD": PART ONE

Lion of Judah... Lamb of God... broken bread and poured out wine... The Word of God is rich with figurative language! Each time God uses simile or metaphor, it is an invitation to imagine. It is an affirmation that He designed the human mind to imagine: that He intends our purposeful use of imagination: that thought, speech, and action ensue from imagination.

It follows that cultivating *moral* thought, speech and action begins by cultivating the *moral* imagination. While only the Holy Spirit quickens us to spiritual vitality, the agents of imagination – story, dance, music, drama, art, poetry – quicken our minds and souls, through our senses, to understand Good and Truth viscerally and authentically, rather than just theoretically. These agents are magic carpets possessing secret passwords into our imaginations; flinging open with one whisper the gates of our hearts; shaping our affections, our expectations, our ability to discern.

Children are not just born with that ability to discern. Discernment develops as the mind and soul, our will and our affections are fed with what C. S. Lewis termed the "savory food" of Good and Truth, guided in both recognition and love of these virtues as distinct from the wicked and the false. The writer of Hebrews explains that "solid food is for the mature, who because of *practice* have their *senses trained* to *discern good and evil*" (Hebrews 5:14, emphasis added).

In other words, merely being born into a Christian family, attending a Christian school or home school, and being imbedded in the context of a church community do not guarantee that we will have had our "senses trained to discern good and evil." They do not guarantee that we will love or acquire virtue. Someone must teach us "This is the fragrance of Goodness! This is the melody of Truth!" and awaken us to their beauty. Then, we must learn and practice skills of observation and analysis, maturing towards discernment in our quest for virtue. This calls for an education – and teachers! – that invite us to proper engagement of the senses, purposeful application of the moral imagination, and many recurring opportunities to explore with creativity God's character, His Word, His world, and our place in it.

Often, even in well-meaning and ostensibly Christian settings, the emphasis is on students' acquisition of data, on delivering information to students who then "give it back" in the form of myriad assessments, on "covering curriculum," or on fostering "Christian behavior," rather than in nurturing those qualities that best equip image-bearers for lifelong learning in loving service to God.

In recent years, the thoroughly atheistic Chinese government has recognized and stated that its people need to develop virtue. It links qualities such as integrity, initiative, independence, creativity and the ability to collaborate with others to China's ability to be competitive in a global economy. Consequently, there has been a proliferation of programs for building character, and a willingness, though perhaps temporary, to invite Western methods and curricula so that their people might adopt those qualities perceived by the government to be valuable. However, as Lewis explains in *The Abolition of Man*, one cannot expect something like virtue to develop where there is neither a common understanding of its definition nor of its source; where the "organ" for virtue (he means the "heart") has been figuratively removed, leaving "men without chests." Vigen Guroian, professor of religious studies at the University of Virgina, asserts in his book, *Tending the Heart of Virtue (1998)*:

> "Mere instruction in morality is not sufficient to nurture the virtues. It might even backfire, especially when the presentation is heavily exhortative and the pupil's will is coerced. Instead, a compelling vision of the goodness of goodness itself needs to be presented in a way that is attractive and stirs the imagination" (p. 20).

This is one way in which things can go quite wrong even in schools and homes that earnestly quest to be "Christian": the teaching of virtue or morality *is* sometimes "heavily exhortative" and the children's wills *may*, in fact, be "coerced," rather than educators' and parents' presenting a winsome invitation into a "compelling vision of the goodness of goodness itself." Sadly, sometimes our approach to teaching virtue is not one that could possibly attract any child, nor stir anyone's imagination. Sometimes "we persist," as

Guroian explains, "in teaching ethics as if it comes from a 'how to' manual for successful living. Moral educators routinely introduce moral principles and even the virtues themselves to students as if they are practical instruments for achieving success" (p. 23).

Does our teaching cultivate the imagination towards virtue? Do our curricula and practices at home and at school properly provide deep immersion in imaginative experiences of Goodness and Truth? Lewis states, "... reason is the natural organ of truth; but imagination is the organ of meaning" (*Mere Christianity*).

Lord, help us learn how to cultivate our children's imaginations to yearn, to desire, to run after virtue!

15 "SAVORY FOOD": PART TWO

C. S. Lewis's poem, with the enigmatic title "On a Theme from Nicolas of Cusa," forms the basis for my description of an integral approach – that is a holistic approach – to educating the imagination toward virtue.

> *When soul and body feed, one sees*
> *Their differing physiologies.*
> *Firmness of apple, fluted shape*
> *Of celery, or tight-skinned grape*
> *I grind and mangle when I eat,*
> *Then, in dark, salt, internal heat,*
> *Annihilate their natures by*
> *The very act that makes them I.*
>
> *But when the soul partakes of good*
> *Or truth, which are her savory food,*
> *By some far subtler chemistry,*
> *It is not they that change, but she,*
> *Who feels them enter with the state*
> *Of conquerors her opened gate,*
> *Or, mirror-like, digests their ray*
> *By turning luminous as they.*

As your eyes read Lewis's poem, your brain was busy, too! The regions identified as Broca's and Wernicke's areas were, of course, doing their job to interpret written words. But it is not only the language-processing parts of your brain that began to light up with activity as you read: the words "grind and mangle" also lit up the motor cortex as if your teeth *were* grinding and mangling, while the descriptions "firmness of apple," and "fluted shape of celery" awakened the neural regions responsible for taste, for gauging the heft of objects, for discerning their texture and their shape. Metaphors describing Good and Truth as "savory food" recalled to your brain other savory foods: rosemary, feta cheese, and garlic; the robust fragrance of your mother's roast beef on returning to your house after church on a Sunday morning. The subsequent metaphor describing Good and Truth as benevolent "conquerors" may recall the return of Aslan to Narnia; the melody of "Pomp and Circumstance" played at graduations, or that of the theme from "Jupiter" in Holst's *The Planets*. Likening the soul's "digestion" of Good and Truth to being "mirror-like" gave your mind a concrete picture for something wholly abstract and set into activity neural connections in multiple parts of your brain. Annie Murphy Paul, in a 2012 New York Times article titled, "Your Brain on Fiction" writes, "The brain, it seems, does not make much of a distinction between reading about an experience and encountering it in real life; in each case, the same neurological regions are stimulated."

When I teach the poem, "On a Theme by Nicolas of Cusa" to 4th and 5th graders, I ask for three volunteers to stand and eat, while the rest of us watch, a bright red apple, a crunchy celery stalk, and a cluster of purple grapes. As these volunteers "grind and mangle" the fruits and vegetables, I playfully invite the audience to observe: "Is Henry turning red like the apple? Is Liz becoming leafy and green like the celery? Is Nolan turning purple like his grapes? Are the kids turning into the foods they are eating?" We laugh – and inevitably, someone will point out that the apple is, in fact, turning into Henry; that the celery is becoming Liz; that the grapes are in the very process of being "annihilated" from their former nature to take on, instead, the nature of Nolan.

Then I read the first stanza of Lewis's poem, and explain that this famous author, who wrote the Narnia Chronicles with which they are so familiar, cared a great deal about food for the body and food for the soul; that in this first stanza he explains something that happens every day and with which we are well-acquainted: our food turns into "us." I ask them to draw a quick sketch on their paper to show what is happening in this first stanza.

At this point, the students have (actually or vicariously) eaten the fruits and vegetable described; they have observed their friends in response to my seemingly serious directive to "watch them carefully"; they have laughed at the absurdity of my suggestion that Susie would take on the aspects of the apple; they are now linking these shared sensory and social experiences with a poem by C. S. Lewis; they are drawing their own conception of what he has described.

When we are ready to engage with the second, and far more abstruse stanza, I alert them to Lewis's cue, the word "but," to ready them for his change of direction, from describing the way our bodies eat to the way our souls "eat" – from physical food to "soul food." I pass around sprigs of fresh rosemary, mint, basil, thyme. As they pinch the leaves, and savor the fragrance, we talk about "savory food." They turn to pair/share with their neighbors about their own favorite "savory foods." They look for and circle the two words that Lewis uses to indicate the savory food on which the soul feeds.

Then I invite them to stand and hold their arms in front of them, with elbows bent and fingers touching, to form a "gate." Two volunteers are chosen to play the characters "Good" and "Truth." Wearing crowns proclaiming these roles, they solemnly process around the room while I play a piece of music that aurally conveys benevolent majesty, such as Rimsky-Korsakov's, "Procession of the Nobles." The other students slowly open their "gates" as Good and Truth approach them.

Music and drama join the array of avenues for sensory experience into which I have invited the students. Can you imagine how many parts of their busy brains have been activated during the course of this engagement with the poem? Sight, smell, taste, as well as humor, role-play, sketching and social interaction contribute to the children's understanding – in a visceral, authentic way – the moral beauty of Good and Truth. They begin to understand how, and with what, they might "feed" their souls. Author Vigen Guroian explains, in his book *Tending the Heart of Virtue: How Classic Stories Awaken a Child's Moral Imagination*, "A good moral education addresses *both* the cognitive and affective dimensions of human nature. Stories are an irreplaceable medium for this kind of moral education – that is, the education of character" (p. 20).

Redemptive Educators: give your children "savory food" at home, at school, at church. Give them story and song, fragrance and flavor, drama and dance, color and line. Pray for their loves to be shaped by His Beauty, His Truth, and His Goodness. Let our homes, our schools, our churches be places of shared delight in the Creator and His glorious creation!

16 "SAVORY FOOD": PART THREE

On autumn, early in the school year on September 11th, when I wanted to share with our K-8 students – almost none of whom had yet been born on 9/11 in 2001 – when I wanted to stir a veneration for the courageous deeds of the heroes of 9/11, I chose a specific outfit to wear and used it as a metaphor in the following way:

I wore a black shirt: black for the danger, loss and grief of that day; black for the darkened hearts of people who had not been taught to love other people; whose souls were clouded with hatred, resentment, violence; black for the remembrance of a national tragedy.

I wore plain beige pants: an unremarkable, common, ordinary color to symbolize the unremarkable, common, and ordinary people whom nobody knew would become heroes that day; people whose selflessness and courage was not flashy or showy or prideful, not obvious in the least until the moment they turned to run towards the danger, to run towards others who needed their help.

I wore a turquoise pendant for the blue, blue sky on that morning of 9/11, when people were heading to work, or off to school, or to the airport to fly through the cloudless, lovely skies.

The turquoise pendant hung on a bright silver chain, and I wore large silver earrings to match: these symbolized the shining "stars" who became heroes that day; whose selflessness and sacrifice saved the lives of others; whose heroic actions continue to shine like silver, like stars in a blue, blue sky.

The children, and the teachers for that matter, were rapt in their attention – I could see in their faces that they took on the sense, as I spoke, of the grievous darkness, the nobility of ordinary citizens rising to courage, the image of the turquoise skies, and veneration for the brightness of heroism. They referenced the impact of the story (and my outfit!) for weeks to follow. Somehow, the visual, sensory experience linked with story had quickened an interior moral experience, the metaphor serving to enliven desire toward virtue.

It was, as we know, the stories of George MacDonald that C. S. Lewis credited with having "baptized" his imagination, long before he actually became a believer in Christ. Stories are powerful venues for cultivating and imparting moral imagination!

David Brooks describes the "road to character" in his eponymous new book highlighting stories of the moral journeys of historic figures such as Augustine, Dwight D. Eisenhower, Dorothy Day and George C. Marshall. In recounting Marshall's education, Brooks writes:

> "[It] taught Marshall a sense of reverence, the imaginative ability to hold up a hero in his mind to copy in all appropriate ways, to let him serve as a standard by which to judge himself ... [I]n the world of Marshall's youth, there was a greater intent to cultivate a capacity for veneration... By cultivating the habit of reverence – for ancient heroes, for the elderly, for leaders in one's own life – teachers were not only offering knowledge of what greatness looks like, they were trying to nurture a talent for admiration. Proper behavior is not just knowing what is right; it is having the motivation to do what is right, an emotion that propels you to do good things" (pp. 107-108)

What kinds of stories do we bring to our children? What kinds of experiences, what kinds of practice do we provide so that their senses might be trained to discern good from evil? So that they might hunger and thirst and desire and quest after the Beautiful, the Good and the True?

I feel deep concern for a generation of children who have been encouraged to enthusiastically sing, "No right, no wrong, no rules for me – I am free!" Can we responsibly affirm their modeling a Disney character whose message presents the casting aside notions of "right" and "wrong" as a proper path towards liberty? We can thank the creators of the movie *Frozen* for inviting us and our children into a few hilarious characters and a few redemptive themes: but we had better also explicitly counter the message of a song that has quickly become the most recognizable and most warmly adopted songs – for children! – of the past few years.

In a book entitled *Fifty Children*, author Steven Pressman recounts the unforgettable experience of an Austrian refugee child rescued from Nazi Germany along with 49 other children, and newly arrived in the United States:

> As the buses meandered through New Jersey and Pennsylvania, Henny Wenkart's first taste of America took on the flavor of inedible chocolate. 'Someone had brought a Whitman's Sampler to the dock, and the box made its way around the bus that I was on,' she remembered. One by one, each of the children bit into the chocolates, which brought at least some of them to tears. 'Viennese chocolate was so good,' Wenkart remembered fondly. 'And the Whitman's chocolates were really awful! (p. 207)

The children's long experience with truly *excellent* chocolate had trained their senses to discern between the high-quality Viennese chocolate and its lesser substitute!

God's word exhorts us:

> Finally, brethren, whatever is true, whatever is honorable, whatever is pure, whatever is lovely, whatever is of good repute, if there is anything excellent or anything worthy of praise, let your mind dwell on these things. The things you have learned and received and heard and seen ... *practice these things*; and the God of peace shall be with you. (Phil. 4:8-9)

Leo Tolstoy likewise exhorts us from his *Pedagogical Articles (1904)*, "In bringing up, educating, developing or ... influencing the child, we ought to have... one aim in view – to attain the greatest harmony possible in the sense of truth, beauty, and goodness" (p. 220).

Let's feed our children "savory food" – let's give them noble stories, rich sensory experiences, interactive creative explorations by means of the arts, songs that sing the Truth into their hearts, so that we might help to educate their imaginations toward virtue.

17 A WEALTH OF WEEDS

Today I went a-walking and noticed a dainty pink flower in abundance along the sidewalk bordering a construction site for yet another crop of apartment buildings in burgeoning Loudoun County. The tiny beads of blossom clustered in a series of rosy spears on slender stems. They caught my eye; I plucked a few stalks to stick in a vase to serve as a subject for my next attempt at watercolor painting. Once I had noticed them, they were everywhere! A wealth of weeds ...

What is a weed? It is something that has sprung up where no one purposed it to be. Persistent in its vigor, it is not a prima donna about conditions: give it a gravelly construction site, a cracked sidewalk, a dusty path, an ever-so-slightly-neglected lawn, a proper flower bed – a weed will find itself at home with a surprising swiftness wherever it may. Undeterred by unpopularity, a weed will cheerfully persevere in threading its roots into complex places, to put forth its prodigal blossoms at every corner. An opportunist, it takes no offense when plucked or pulled, but merely reappears in the subsequent square foot of soil.

My newfound weed was winsome: it invited research. Wikipedia and other helpful sources were unanimous in their opinion that my posies were a knotweed. And edible! (Well – according to Wikipedia – "especially in a famine.") A renegade member of the sensible buckwheat family, the knotweed scatters her wee black seeds to propagate in season and out. I am impressed.

She is not the only weed out there, of course. Once my eye is awakened, it discovers foxtail, a delicate grass flower you've seen a million times without noticing. There is crown vetch, objectionably invasive, who nonetheless pours her nitrogen into any soil who will receive her. She cannot help the fact that she tends to take over the world. Dainty bells of blossom, pink and white, remind us that she is a member of the pea family, and I find her sweet. She may take over my neck of the woods anytime she likes – she brings improvement, I think, to the abandoned railroad track or the compromised corner of a junkyard.

Who else might I discover if only my eyes are trained to see? Who might I find if only I learn to notice?

18 SEVENTH, EIGHTH, AND BEETHOVEN'S NINTH

Our seventh and eighth graders are learning how to be revolutionaries – and how *not* to be revolutionaries! Questing after God's call in their lives means seeing the world through a biblical framework – a framework radically "other" than that which our culture provides. It requires a revolutionary outlook, one that asks:

- What was God's original intent for _____ (music, literature, society)?
- Where, and to what extent, do we see that original intent reflected in our study of _____ (Bach's chorales, Macbeth, British monarchy)?
- Where, and to what extent, do we see evidence of "the fall of man" reflected in our study of _____ (Beethoven's 9th Symphony, the Constitution, Robespierre)?
- How is God calling me/us to respond to all of the above? In what ways does He invite me/us into His ongoing redemptive work in the world?

These young scholars are learning to apply this framework to everything in which they engage, whether as part of their formal curriculum, or the "curriculum of life" – friendships, aspirations, use of time and other resources, choice of activities and avocations, exploring God's world and discovering their place in it.

In seminar, they will continue a "dialogue" with none other than Ludwig van Beethoven, who has been sharing his perspectives on "revolutions" by means of his Ninth Symphony. The first movement paints a picture of conflagration, chaos, and conquest – we "hear" the pounding of cannons, a march to the gallows (or perhaps the guillotine?), the tumbling of buildings, the shock of cacophony, the shock of dead silence – and through his music, we understand from Beethoven the consequences related to one approach to bringing about change, one approach to "revolution."

The second movement features a different facet of "revolution" – we "hear" conspiracy, collusion, confidential conversations suddenly interrupted – and all the anxious activity, the sneaking around, the hopeful interludes curtailed by an unexpected "boom!" – by which Beethoven helps us understand another aspect of bringing about change in a dangerous world.

We rest as Beethoven's third movement invites us to contemplate the change we hope for, to listen for where ideas find confluence, to discern the flow of activity beneath a seemingly-serene surface of events.

Finally, Beethoven will startle us out of any complacency regarding revolution. He will lead us in consideration – and rejection – of his first three ideas as presented in the previous movements. He will tell us: *Might does NOT make right! (movement #1) All the anxious activity in the world may not be able to effect lasting change! (movement #2) Merely dreaming about utopia is insufficient if you want to be a world-changer! (movement #3).* Beethoven will make his case for building consensus, uniting as brothers, and joyfully marching ever upward towards a world of triumphant gladness, singing the "Ode to Joy."

Then: we do the crucial work of putting these ideas through the biblical worldview filter, the four questions posed above. What is God's intent for the world? Which parts of Beethoven's musical ideas reflect God's intent for His beautiful world? Where, and to what extent, does Beethoven reflect (intentionally or otherwise) the fact of sin and error in the world?

And – most important – How is God calling us, calling me – to respond, to participate in His work of loving the world and reconciling it to Himself?

This is the work of revolutionaries! Be praying for our young "world-changers"!

19 SIMPLICITY SCHOOLING

Recently, a mom asked if we could meet to discuss strategies for finding a sustainable simplicity in her parenting. Knowing that there would surely be other moms and dads in our midst questing for the same outcomes in their homes, we decided to set up a few informal gatherings to share ideas and support this effort. Coincidentally, someone gifted me with a book entitled, *Simplicity Parenting: Using the Extraordinary Power of Less to Raise Calmer, Happier, and More Secure Kids*, which, although not written from a biblical worldview perspective, nevertheless aligns in many key aspects with our thoughts on nurturing the uniqueness of each child, facilitating development of sound character, and a holistic approach to all things pertaining to the raising of children.

The authors of the book, Lisa M. Ross and Kim John Payne, beautifully and skillfully articulate what the embracing of simplicity contributes to the wellbeing of children and families. They describe the best kinds of toys to provide for imaginative play, the sorts of activities most conducive to the cultivation of creativity and patterns for daily living that are likeliest to promote a peaceful home.

A redemptive education seeks to bring health to a learning community in which persons, programs, and perspectives are fractured and frazzled, the casualties of too much division, adrenaline, and resultant exhaustion. Our children need this healing. We need it, too! We cannot escape the escalation of pressure and the demand for increasing involvements in the hundreds of "good things" available for us and for our children, unless we purposefully and prayerfully determine to swim against that tide in our homes and in our schools.

Each year, and throughout the year, let's think deeply about the programs we undertake, the schedules we maintain, the degree of "white space" we enjoy (or lack!) in the regular structures of our units of study and in our home and school events. Let's quest together for a life at school and at home that includes rhythms of focused engagement and rest, human "doing" and human "being." Our ideal is a framework in which a blessed predictability provides enough flexibility to chase after children's initiatives, to follow possible paths and see what we discover, to dream and to dialogue, as well as to master our multiplication tables and the Latin conjugations of the verb *esse* ("to be").

In the words of the old Shaker hymn, "'Tis a gift to be simple, 'tis a gift to be free!" Let's explore a deeper understanding of the connection between simplicity and freedom in the scriptural encouragement from 2 Cor 3:17, "Now the Lord is Spirit, and where the Spirit of the Lord is, there is liberty!"

20 PONDERINGS FROM THE BERRY PATCH

When berries are ripe, they are easy to pick.

The ripest berries are often hidden beneath the leaves – they are not always immediately evident.

In any cluster of berries, you find a whole range of readiness for harvesting: the green are mixed in with the pink are mixed in with the deep purple.

If you keep looking around for the "best" berries, you miss the ones right in front of you.

You cannot possibly pick ALL the berries. You cannot reach them all.

Picking berries involves getting purple stains on your fingers and having to dodge briars.

It is better to move carefully, to avoid getting tangled in briars, than it is to try to get unsnagged after having been careless. Take your time. Be strategic.

If you eat the berries, you *will* get blackberry seeds in your teeth along with all the sweetness.

Sometimes the berries are sour – tart! But those make the best jam.

If you come back to the berry patch in just a few days, you will find more fruit for the harvest.

21 ALL NATURE SINGS!

"All nature sings!" and so do we, every morning in our chapel time. We sing the heritage hymns of the Christian faith more often than contemporary choruses simply because our children typically have so little exposure now to great classics such as "This is my Father's World," "Be Thou my Vision," and our current favorite of a very different flavor, "Bringing in the Sheaves."

Knowles Shaw, or "Brother Shaw" as he was affectionately called, who wrote the words for "Bringing in the Sheaves," was also known as the "Singing Evangelist." He evidently wrote numerous hymns for use in his 19 years' worth of evangelistic services, about which he said, " Oh, it is a grand thing to rally people to the Cross of Christ!" Those were, in fact, his last words before his sudden death in a train accident while on his way to yet another city to preach the gospel.

Brother Shaw's hymn illuminates many of the big ideas with which we have been engaging in our devotional considerations together each morning. From our initial discussions of blackberries, we moved to discussions of wheat berries, with some fun observations thrown in for good measure. Who could have guessed that old wheat grain, suffering silently from neglect in the back of my freezer for several years, would sprout, when given half a chance, into the swiftest growing plants ever spotted in our school?! What a thrill for our students to see for themselves that something that lay dormant for many a year may spring into life just as soon as conditions are right – plenty of metaphors to be had in that little experiment.

The very concrete experience of seeing "dead" wheat berries produce green sprouts also enlarges our understanding of Jesus' metaphor: Unless a grain of wheat falls into the earth and dies, it remains by itself alone – but if it dies, it bears much fruit! Aaahhhh... now we get it! We had to see it to "get it"!

Our discussions each morning about Brother Shaw's lyrics, and the many accompanying conversations, give us opportunity also to grow in our ability to "summarize" and to "expand upon" others' ideas. From kindergarten through eighth grade, we practice listening to peers, colleagues, and ourselves attempt to articulate complex notions. Then we see if we might give a succinct summary of that articulation, or whether we might take that idea and build upon it to deepen our understanding of its implications.

This is "thinking work" for sure. You might want to pick up this practice at home, around your table or during your commute, inviting your children or offering your own attempts to distill complex concepts, or to augment and develop statements in order to reflect levels of sophistication that had not previously been recognized. (Please do not think I am suggesting a lot of self-consciously shared "fancy language" – oh, no! Keep it all simple, keep it authentic – even complicated ideas may be talked about with simplicity – note the work of C. S. Lewis, for example.)

Summarizing, expanding upon – this is very good thinking work. So is
"creating." While exploring the idea that "all nature sings" we began to wonder together: If a stone could sing, what might it sing? And together, we wrote such a lovely beginning to ... to what? a poem? a song? It starts like this:

> *I am Stone.*
> *I sing of stability and strength,*
> *I sing of streams ...*

22 COME, YE THANKFUL PEOPLE, COME!

Come, ye thankful people, come,
Raise the song of harvest home!
All is safely gathered in,
Ere the winter storms begin;
God, our Maker, doth provide
All our wants to be supplied;
Come to God's own temple, come;
Raise the song of harvest home!

All the world is God's own field,
Fruit unto His praise to yield;
Wheat and tares together sown
Unto joy or sorrow grown;
First the blade and then the ear,
Then the full corn shall appear;
Lord of harvest, grant that we
Wholesome grain and pure may be.

When he wasn't doing half a hundred other interesting things (translating *The Odyssey*, chiseling the frontispiece for a pipe organ, lecturing, preaching, studying German, painting watercolors, or writing novels with his niece) Henry Alford (1810-1871), fifth generation British Anglican priest wrote poetry and lyrics such as the verses shown above.

Our children have been making connections between the ideas of "sowing" and "reaping," of actual and metaphorical "seed" and "fruit" and "harvest." They have, together with teachers and parents, been meditating on these significant metaphors from which Jesus taught essential ideas to His disciples and other listeners.

Parents and teachers: you have been "sowing"! Whether cognizant or not of your occupation as a "sower," you have been effectively sowing all sorts of things into the fertile ground of your children's minds and hearts. In the same passage in 2 Corinthians chapter nine in which we are encouraged to sow bountifully, we are also reminded that God loves a cheerful giver. Hmmm...

Are we cheerful in our giving? I don't mean dollars and cents, although certainly that is part of what St. Paul must have had in mind. But I am thinking now of "giving" in the sense that you "give" of yourselves constantly, morning to afternoon to evening and (parents!) often through the night as you care for and cultivate the young lives entrusted to you. You are, most certainly, "sowing seeds of kindness" and also "seeds" of intellect, of curiosity, of yearning for God, of selflessness, of humility, of perseverance, of truthfulness, of diligence, of love.

But you are not harvesting yet. You sometimes see sprouts or encouraging signs of growth and potential fruitfulness. You might see reasons to hope that the young plants have started well. The Great Harvest will come in the future. We have hours and days and weeks and months and years – probably decades! - of "sowing" to do before that Great Harvest time arrives. So how do we keep on "sowing"?

Immediately following Paul's exhortation in 2 Cor. 9:7 regarding being "cheerful givers," he encourages us with some important information on how to persevere in that cheerful giving:

> And GOD is able to make *all grace abound* to you, so that having *all* sufficiency in *all* things at *all* times, you may *abound* in *every* good work... *He* who supplies seed for sowing and bread for food will supply and multiply *your* seed for sowing and increase the harvest of your righteousness. You will be enriched in every way to be generous in every way... (2 Cor. 9: 9a, 10-11a, emphasis added)

If we pay attention to the italicized words in the passage above, and meditate on their implications, we find the secret weapon to consistently, constantly giving cheerfully as parents, as teachers, as board members: It is GOD who is able! He makes the grace abound, He enables YOU to abound in every good work (translate: washing, tidying, praying, shopping, driving, disciplining, feeding, washing, tidying ...) for this lifelong service as a "cheerful giver."

He not only supplies the seeds for you to sow, but He promises also to feed YOU, the "sower," as you work and work and work. He promises to bring about increase in the "harvest" of your righteousness in Christ – and from that we can derive confidence that He will not neglect to bring about increase in the "harvest" of all those many investments you are making every hour, day, week, year, decade as you "sow" into the lives of your precious children. Sow generously! Then – be patient. He is the Lord of the Harvest!

23 WHITE SPACE

Lonely, isolated child spends years in the protected environment of her own home and gardens. She draws, she paints, she invents her own secret code with which to write in her journal. Her governess allows her to pursue her fascination with the flora and fauna in her own backyard.

"Thank goodness my education was largely neglected and the originality was not rubbed out!" -- Beatrix Potter

Useless schoolboy is sent home to be taught by his mother, as the teacher proclaims him "addled." Eventually, he gets a degree, but cannot seem to land a real job. At last, he is awarded a "dead end" position in a patent office, doing brainless work which requires no effort. The next seven years are the most intellectually productive of his life.

"The monotony and solitude of a quiet life stimulate the creative mind." – Albert Einstein

What did these two most prolific and brilliant of people have in common? A lot of time. Time when they were not doing a hundred other magnificent things. No play dates, no soccer, no girl scouts, no karate, no piano lessons, no AWANAs, no choir, no baseball, no tv, no movies, no games.

According to Einstein, the creative mind must have some measure of (dare we believe him?) monotony. Solitude. And a quiet life. "White space" – when no one is telling you what to do, what to think, how to play, where to go, what to make - and the mind is left alone with itself and its ideas.

Well: we wouldn't dream of neglecting education! We would never advocate idleness! And monotony? God forbid! We exist to stimulate, stir, inform and delight. Joyously we gallop through our days, in pursuit of the highest and the best.

Our very strength may become our weakness if we are not thoughtful about these things. After all, both Paul and Timothy urge us to "make it your ambition to lead a quiet life," and "lead a tranquil and quiet life."

As we meditate on the theme "I Rest Me," let us make sure that we ask ourselves a vital question: Do our children have time to think? Do we?

"I think and think for months and years. Ninety-nine times, the conclusion is false. The 100th time, I am right." - - Albert Einstein

"The only thing that interfered with my learning was my education."
"It is a miracle that curiosity survives formal education!" – Albert Einstein

Can curiosity survive formal education? And if so, how?

As people dedicated to the education of children, it is worth our time to consider the question!

24 SOME THINGS TAKE TIME

1905: the Wonder Year! The Annus Mirabilis of the young man who, having struggled to pass university exams, who having tried unsuccessfully to secure a teaching position, who having taken an inconsequential job at the patent office, produced four of the most revolutionary ideas of the modern world. This young man's school career certainly had not been stellar. It was marked by extremes of failure and achievement, conflict with professors, uncertainty of success. But when Albert Einstein took on the dull job of reviewing patent applications, his brilliant mind was busy behind the scenes, resulting in the development of his surprising theories on the topics of light, space, time and matter.

Harper Lee, born in 1926, based her 1962 Pulitzer Prize winning first novel, To Kill a Mockingbird on events and people she had known a quarter of a century earlier. It is considered a true masterpiece, perfect in its character development, its plot, its language, and its portrayal of a particular time and place. Although she is still alive today, Lee's novel stands not only as her magnum opus, but her only "opus"; she never wrote another book. (*The recent publication of a controversial "prequel" was discovered and released after the writing of this article... certainly, it does not compete with To Kill a Mockingbird as "magnum opus".)

Father Abraham has a son. Isaac in turn has a son named Jacob. Jacob spends most of his youth tussling with his brother, deceiving his father, dreaming of angels, and hearing divine directives. But not until he's a middle-aged man does he wrestle with an angel, get a new name, and finally cry "El-Elohe-Israel!" or "God, the God of Israel!" What took him so long?

Well, some things take time. Even when God is powerfully at work, speaking to us, rescuing us, blessing us, it can take a long time before we believe and receive. Even when we pour ourselves wholeheartedly into some good work, some great quest, some worthy cause, the fruits may be shockingly variable in their time of arrival, their extent, or their effect. Was Harper Lee any less remarkable an author for having written "only" one book? But what a book!

The prolific Kentucky poet-farmer, Wendell Berry, writes a Sabbath poem every Sunday of every week of every year and has done so for the past number of decades. His book A Timbered Choir, presents some of these poems from each year spanning 1979 to 1997. However, for the year 1986, only a single poem is given. We know he wasn't twiddling his thumbs on all those Sabbaths in 1986; we know he was faithfully, devotionally, writing, writing, writing poems – yet evidently, only a single poem made the cut to be included in that volume. Only one "good" poem out of a possible 52? Not such a great "average output," one might think. So – was he wasting his time all those other Sundays?

Yes, some things take time. Ideas, stories, poems, faith: these often require vast expanses of hours, days, years and lifetimes before the "magnum opus" appears. There are often false starts. Aspiring writers might be heartened to see the number of failed beginnings E.B. White produced before he landed on the compelling beginning of his book, Charlotte's Web: "'Where's Papa going with that ax?' said Fern to her mother" ... (If this interests you, see The Annotated Charlotte's Web to read some of his insipid first attempts, including "Charlotte was a big grey spider." The book also gives background on the fascinating interaction between White and his famous illustrator, Garth Williams.)

Here's another thing that takes time: educating a person. Life-long learners – that's what we're trying to develop at home and at school, from the children to the teachers to the parents to the Board to the Head of School – a community of life-long learners rejoicing together, laboring together, exploring God's wonderful world together and finding our place in it.

As summer approaches, take a little time – to read, to lounge, to think, to plan, to converse, to garden, to hike, to swim, to toast marshmallows. I can't promise it will yield revolutionary new scientific theories, or a Pulitzer Prize-winning novel, or even a single poem – but Lord willing it will yield a sense of wonder, gratitude, and worship in your family's journey of faith.

25 SUPER KID

Look out, parents. There's a monster out there called "SuperKid" and I'm just letting you know. All over the world, parents are discovering that their super-parenting is churning out SuperKids, and it's not a pretty picture.

According to Carl Honore, author of *Under Pressure: Rescuing Our Children from the Culture of Hyper-Parenting*, 400,000 Japanese Superkids have opted to become fulltime hermits, known as *hikikomori*. They do not come out of their rooms. They would rather hunker down in hungry solitude than face the relentless stress of performance expectations. Honore also reports, "In Brittany, France, anxiety and suicide rates have risen in tandem with rising marks in the tough baccalauréat exams and greater access to higher education." (p. 10)

Yong Zhao, founding director of the U.S. – China Center for Research on Educational Excellence expresses deep concern in his new book *Catching Up or Leading the Way: American Education in the Age of Globalization*. He writes that in his native China, where the number-one killer of people between the ages of 15 and 34 is suicide, pressure to excel academically and get into university is linked with a vast number of these deaths. Chinese parents begin the quest to develop their children into SuperKids during their earliest years. Every Chinese school, preschool through high school, is fixated on preparing its students to pass the *gaokao*, the comprehensive graduation exam, with flying colors. Chinese parents who can afford it, and many who cannot, will rent an apartment, move their adolescent in, and wait on the scholar hand and foot during the intensive study period leading up to the *gaokao*. Heaven help the teen and his parents if the test does not go well. How can they return to their homes and neighbors with such a blot on their reputation? They may never live down the shame associated with failure on this test.

But SuperKids are homegrown on our continent, too. Honore shares one of his favorite *New Yorker* cartoons:

> It depicts two little girls waiting for the school bus, each holding a personal planner. One tells the other, "Okay, I'll move ballet back an hour, reschedule gymnastics and cancel piano ... You shift your violin lessons to Thursday and skip soccer practice ... That gives us from 3:15 p.m. to 3:45 p.m. on Wednesday the 16th to play." (p. 162)

Funny, if it weren't so close to being true.

In Chapter 8 of *Under Pressure*, titled "Extracurricular Activities: Ready, Set, Relax!" Honore tells of a pediatrician in Ridgewood, NJ who claims that:

> 65 percent of his patients are now the victims of overscheduling. He says the symptoms include headaches, sleep disorders, gastric problems caused by stress or by eating too late at night, and fatigue. "Fifteen years ago it was unusual to see a tired ten-year-old," he quotes the physician, "Now it's common." (p. 168)

Why do we do this? Why do we wear out ourselves and our children by immersing them in the dozens of opportunities available to them? Because we love our kids and we want them to succeed. We want to open every possible door for their futures. And sometimes, we lose perspective. Honore quotes a fourteen-year-old girl who complains, "I feel like a project that my parents are always working on." He goes on to explain, "We all suffer when children become projects. Instead of bringing families together, too much striving and rushing around can end up pulling them apart."

One night, we spent a profitable evening together discussing Richard Louv's thought-provoking book, *Last Child in the Woods: Saving Our Children from Nature-Deficit Disorder*. We know our kids are super – we don't need to turn them into SuperKids. But the press of our culture and our good intentions may get the better of us if we are not equally intentional about preserving some quietness in the lives of our children, allowing them time to reflect, to imagine, to play – and time just to "be." (Recently, a mother told me, "I think my child actually IS the 'last child in the woods!' Every time we invite friends over to play, they can't come because they have soccer, or piano, or AWANAs or baseball or tutoring! No one has time to play!")

We care about parenting our children! We must actively, and purposefully resist the temptation to make them our projects. Can we trust the Lord to shape them and their futures according to His plan, without our fretful and perpetual intervention?

.

26 FLAWED AND INSUFFICIENT

Have you ever had to empty a little boy's pockets? What did you find? A silly band ... a Lego piece ... a sparkly stone ... a disintegrating biscuit from breakfast two days ago ... yikes! That biscuit, which emerged from your oven last Tuesday - fragrant, flaky, ready for butter and marmalade - is now half a brown brick and a bunch of crumbles. Hard. Stale. A home for those bacteria which live in little boys' pockets.

Just be glad you didn't find a fish! When Jesus and His disciples faced an immense crowd of hungry people, their resources consisted of five loaves of bread and two fishes that a boy had been hoisting around (in his pockets?) for who-knows-how-long. They could not have been "germ-free." They were certainly not packaged hygienically. The items at hand were dirty, cold, and wholly insufficient for the needs of five thousand people.

The Sunday School lesson which all of us learned long ago is true: Jesus is able to take a "little" and make it "a lot." He takes "not enough" and transforms it into "more than enough." But the lesson which only recently presented itself to me is slightly different: Jesus is able to take very flawed material - not merely insufficient, but deeply flawed - and cause it to become a source of blessing and nourishment to others. He takes what is brought to Him - dirty, crumbled, stale - and breathes such life and grace and goodness into it that it becomes food for many, a feast around which we gather in delight.

"Flawed and insufficient" - This is how we come to school. Teachers, students, Board members, office staff, Head of School - we arrive each morning both flawed and insufficient for the duties of the day. We are the Fellowship of the Flawed, and we bring what we have to the Lord of All Mercy, the Lord of All Power, who takes our loaves and fishes and somehow makes them "enough," "more than enough," "nutritious," and "delicious." This is His doing entirely - and so we give thanks.

Over thirty years ago a young seminarian and his wife were evaluated by their mission board in order to receive their overseas assignment. They had China on their minds and hearts and had studied hard to prepare for a life of ministry in that part of the globe. When the evaluation came back from the mission board, the report read as follows: "In considering this couple's request for assignment in China, the committee has concluded that their liabilities outweigh their potential."

What a devastating pronouncement! It drove the young couple to soul-searching prayer, to further counsel, and finally, to the decision that they would go to China one way or another and fulfill their calling from God. They packed their bags with both liabilities and potential - and set off for what turned out to be a long career in ministry with Chinese populations, in Taiwan as well as in the US. Andy Pigott currently serves as one of the pastors of the Chinese Christian Church of New Jersey, and recently recounted this story at the State College, PA Alliance Church, where thirty years ago I heard him preach on the topic of "Our Liabilities Outweigh Our Potential."

We're all in the same boat. Any good fruit that comes from our lives, as parents, as educators, as learners, as trustees, comes from the transforming hand of the Good Shepherd. Let's be faithful to pray for one another - Let's show grace to one another. We are flawed and insufficient - but He is great, able to multiply loaves and fishes, able to take us as we are when we present ourselves to Him, able to bring about wonderful things as we commit our way to Him, as we delight ourselves in Him. May our homes and our schools always be places of delight, of learning, of earnest service and love for God and for one another.

27 COLORING INSIDE THE LINES

I was a guest in a faraway church. Surrounded by warm and welcoming smiles, encouraged by seeing two beloved hymns listed in the bulletin, I had no idea that I was about to witness the worst children's sermon I'd ever heard. It was delivered, with love, by a nice Christian lady to the one poor child, a boy of about 8 years old, who'd had the misfortune of having shown up in the 11:00 service that morning. Mrs. Nice Christian Lady (NCL) held in her soft hands a Barbie coloring book and a fat red crayon.

It was bad enough for the Embarrassed Boy (EB) to find himself summoned, alone, to the front of the sanctuary in the evident absence of peers. (Clearly, the other children knew to dodge the 11:00 service; perhaps this pitiable child was someone's visiting grandson and had not been warned.) To make matters worse, as the stricken EB slumped, blushing, on the chancel steps, facing Mrs. NCL and the offensive Barbie, he was charged with responding to the following query: "Do you know what this is?"

"A girl coloring book," he mumbled.

"That's right! It's a coloring book!" was her cheery and enthusiastic reply. "Do you like to color?" EB looked distraught. "Well, when you first learned to color, did you color outside the lines?"

"Yes," he mumbled again, and turned away to stare hard at a far corner of the carpet.

"Of course you did! Everybody colors outside the lines when they're little, but then they learn how to color inside the lines, right?" EB kept staring at the corner of the carpet. "But now that you're bigger, I bet you could color this picture really nicely, right? You wouldn't go out of the lines at all, would you. Well, the Bible is like the rule book for coloring life. In the Bible, God tells us what we need to do to stay inside the lines, right? By the time you're a grown up, you won't scribble outside the lines like you did when you were little, right? And if you follow God's rule book as you grow up, you'll get better and better at staying in the lines when you're 'coloring life,' right? And that's what God wants us to do, isn't it? He wants us to work hard to make sure we're always coloring inside the lines. And that's our children's sermon for today."

With that, EB slunk back to his pew while the benevolent crowd sang, "Jesus Loves Me, This I Know."

Now, there are so many things wrong with that scenario it is hard to know where to begin. But I would probably do well to start with two positive observations. Mrs. NCL was warm and friendly; we know she meant well. And perhaps she did no harm. After all, her audience consisted of only one child, one reluctant boy who did not appear to be receptive to her message. We can hope that she did no harm.

But what if that child had actually believed her! What if he succumbed to the unwieldy weight of responsibility for a lifetime of "coloring inside the lines"? What if he (God forbid) accidentally made a mark outside the lines? Or worse: What if, in some blind moment of hot anger, he picked up that red crayon and scribbled all over the page, all over that Barbie and altogether outside of the lines?!

And worse again: What if he had an idea for a drawing – something unrelated to Barbie, or heavy black lines, or even a red crayon? What if this child, made in God's image, had God-given images dancing in his brain? What if those images danced right down his arms, and through his eager fingers into soft brown clay? What if he shaped surprising creatures, or life-like figures or a rounded clay bowl? What if he needed, instead, a large canvas, bright paints, and a thick bristled brush? Or a stack of rainbow colored papers to fold and crease and transform into origami cranes?

There is so much more for a child to know than the burdensome necessity (unnecessary) of perpetually coloring inside the lines. Pity the poor child who is never told, "You were made in the image of the Great Artist! He invites you to celebrate His gifts of color, shape, line, shadow – aren't they lovely? Aren't they so rich! Come be a co-adventurer with the Creator of amethyst, the pen-and-ink Sketcher of tree limbs at dusk, the Painter of turtles, the Sculptor of boulders, the Weaver of spider webs, the Scatterer of stars! Stay near Him – for there you find fragrance and music and blessing! He is the One who brings beauty from ashes, who turns the gray dirges to songs of great joy! And if (God have mercy) you blunder past parameters, *outside the lines* – here is happy news: *There is a Redeemer, Jesus, God's own Son! Precious Lamb of God, Messiah, Holy One!*"

28 SONGS AND STORIES, STORIES AND SONGS

When a visitor asked a small student what she learned at school that day, the child said, "Songs and stories. Stories and songs." Concise, and probably accurate! Whether the class is studying fractions, grammar, simple machines or the Civil War, you are very likely to hear them singing or see them listening intently to some narrative related to the topic.

Why *do* Redemptive Educators spend so much time with "songs and stories ... stories and songs"? Shouldn't they be busy educating our children in important matters such as multiplication? Forms of government? Cursive writing? Doctrines of the faith? Yes, yes, yes, and of course, yes!

But the God who is both our Savior and our Great Teacher has also seen fit to reveal Himself to us through songs and stories, stories and songs. He calls Himself "the author and finisher of our faith," and He gives us "songs in the night." He causes the stars to sing, He commands His people to "make melody in their hearts to God," and to continually tell the generations the story of His faithfulness and His mighty deeds.

God, as you might guess, is not unaware of how powerfully music, literature, and all of the arts influence our minds and hearts. Beautiful language linked with melody and harmony can shape the layers of our intellects and of our souls. And so we sing scripture. We sing "Be Thou My Vision, O Lord of my Heart!" We sing the "Addition Toughies" and "The Continents and Oceans" and of course, "My Country, 'Tis of Thee." A song will keep lyrics deeply imbedded in our brains for decades upon decades. (This is why my husband sometimes finds himself singing, "Oh, I wish I were an Oscar Meyer Weiner, That is what I'd really like to be, 'Cause if I were an Oscar Meyer Weiner, Everyone would be in love with me!" On a more serious note, late in a night spent by the bed of a sick child, when I longed to cease vigil and find my own bed, I discovered to my dismay that the song going through my head was an ancient Burt Bacharach classic urging me to "make it easy on yourself ..." – not a helpful concept at that moment.)

God is the original Plot Maker, who designed a setting, characters, conflict, climax and resolution in the original and still-unfolding Story. Astonishingly, He invites each one of us to participate in the details of this plot, and the development of at least one "main character" – ourselves! By means of story, the abstract but imperative concepts of courage, sacrifice, liberty, faith, hope and love are made concrete through the words and deeds of Jean Valjean or Joni Eareckson Tada, Hudson Taylor or Anne of Green Gables, Reepicheep or Robin Hood.

Not only is our God the creator of story and song, He is also the original mathematician, the original chemist, the original engineer and the original economist. He is Lord of biology and bioethics, geography and geometry, physics and philosophy. Here's a song about the original choreographer:

I danced in the morning when the world was begun!
I danced in the moon and the stars and the sun!
I came down from heaven and I danced on the earth -
At Bethlehem, I had my birth!
Dance, then, wherever you may be!
I am the Lord of the dance, said He,
And I'll lead you all wherever you may be,
And I'll lead you all in the dance, said He. (lyrics by Sydney Carter)

29 A WORD ABOUT WRITING

I had a funny experience this week. A publication arrived on my desk and I began to read it. As I read, I found myself pleased with the author's use of language. I found myself nodding in appreciation for the ideas and their expression; I was struck by the degree to which it resonated with my own thoughts and feelings. Eventually, there came a strange, slow "knowing" – I had written it.

Doubting myself, (it was not cited), I checked my computer for a document from several years ago: sure enough, there it was, word for word! I was the author! No wonder it resonated with my own thoughts and feelings: it *was* my own thoughts and feelings. But what a strange realization – as if I had looked for long moments at a photo of myself, without recognizing my own face.

Writing can certainly take on a life of its own. But it always starts in the mind of a writer. It has a long and perilous journey to travel, from the heart and the brain of some person, down the arm to the fingers, which pick up a pen or open a laptop and place the first tentative words on a page.

Our school has approximately 100 "writers in residence," including board members, parents, teachers, and vast numbers of children who have things to say. We are joyful and reverent participants in the process of learning to "speak" through the written word, in essays, reports, poems, stories and letters. But how in the world do we go about it?

A.A. Milne says in his poem "When we were One, we had just begun ..." and how true this is for the students! At first, the great task is to learn those letters, their sounds, their formations, and lots of tricky ways they like to arrange themselves into words. We begin to make the connection between those loops and dots and lines and spaces and all the stories we hear and tell. Young scholars read and write haiku, fractured fairytales, and information about trees. The great goal is to establish the foundational principle that writing is for US, each one of us – as readers, as writers, as people who have things to communicate and are eager to share with others.

This laying of foundations continues as students grow older: spelling of words that follow the rules, some sight words who are "rule-breakers," the inevitability of capitals and periods, and the fancy addition of cursive penmanship. These primary grades are where the elementary tools of writing are acquired, and love for language is cultivated. First, we just get the "juices flowing." Then come the beginning of expectations for self and peer editing, focused on one or two aspects of a few written assignments, with continued emphasis on joyful participation in the process. These are eventually accompanied by growing attention to editing, length and frequency of writing assignments, and bringing a few pieces to a final finished product.

In sometime around fourth grade or age nine marks the transition into more "grown up" writing. The emphases include increasingly complex basic grammar, punctuation, the construction of paragraphs and a fluency with legible writing, especially in cursive. Students take preliminary steps in learning how to organize information, research a topic, write lengthier papers with sub-headings, and express their ideas with effectiveness.

Sixth grade, or around age eleven, is a developmentally strong time to begin exploring three categories of writing: expressive, persuasive, and expository. Sixth graders are ready for larger participation in events and contests such as the "River of Words" poetry contest. This gives practice in conforming to external standards, while developing thinking and writing in metaphor and figurative language. Students can put persuasive writing to work in representing a point of view; seeking to effect response from local, state and federal leaders; eliciting action within the school and the greater community. Expository and technical writing can be key components of the science curriculum during the sixth-grade year, and students can gain practice in clear communication of information and its analysis.

The seventh and eighth grade years of a student's education should include a marked focus on skillful writing of every kind. Twelve and thirteen-year olds are ready to begin thinking deeply and writing thoughtfully about their faith, their calling, the journey they are embarked on to explore God's world and find their place in it. As they develop into young adults during the high school years, allow (and require) both a broad range of types of writing, *and* the time and space for a "deep dive" into a genre or two of the students' choice.

And, oh yes ... you might want to teach them not to plagiarize. ☺

30 CONNECTIONS

Integral curriculum is all about connections: connections between events, facts, observations, ideas and actions. Some years ago, when first and second graders were studying "rest, sleep, and sabbath in God's world," they discovered during their morning recess a pair of snoozing salamanders under a rock outside. What a surprise! The little creatures woke from their dream (their nightmare!) and scuttled away as fast as they could. We scuttled inside to "look them up" and found out all sorts of interesting things, including the fact that our "salamanders" were actually newts.

"What do they do under that rock all winter long?" the children wondered. "We didn't even know they were there!"

Later, the painted lady caterpillars gobbled their way through the food provided, hung from a thread, and hardened into pupae. "What are they doing in there?" the children wanted to know. "Are they still alive? It looks like nothing's happening!"

A trip to Domino Pizza and some school-baked bread helped our students understand the action of yeast. "How can that powder make the bread dough poof up?" asked the young scientists. We made some without the yeast and noted the significant difference, even though at first, both batches of dough looked exactly alike.

The lovely music of Faure's "After a Dream" and the story and music from "A Midsummer Night's Dream" became familiar friends to the dancing first and second graders. They also read bedtime stories and listened to lullabies and nocturnes. They could identify "Moonlight Sonata" and "Claire de Lune" and paint Van Gogh's stars.

"Be still and know that I am God," we sang in morning chapel. "In returning and rest you will be saved," we read, "in quietness and trust shall be your strength." (Isaiah 30:16) "Stand still and see the salvation of the Lord!" (Exodus 14:13) "Remember the

70

Sabbath to keep it holy." (Exodus 20:8) the students copied into their Narration Station notebooks.

How does sleeping help us to grow? How do butterflies come out from a hard, brown shell? What's so strong about quietness and trust? How can standing still result in salvation? What does it mean to "remember the Sabbath"? How many days are from one Sabbath to the next?

Who keeps us safe when we sleep at night? Why do we dream? How many hours of sleep do we need? Where do the various animals sleep? What is hibernation? How does God "give to His beloved even in [their] sleep"? (Ps. 127:2)

Integral study is lifelong study. We cannot exhaust the wonders of even one single aspect of God's creation, nor can we uncover the full extent of its unity with the whole. What a joyful and fascinating endeavor for us all, to be co-adventurers in discovering an ever widening, ever deepening understanding of this magnificent world and its Maker.

Eventually, those same students who surprised the newts sang "their" song to a class of younger students:

Under a stone (where it looks like nothing's happening)
Two little newts take their winter nap!
Under the snow (where we can't tell that it's happening)
All of the trees are filling up with sap!
When we're asleep (and it looks like nothing's happening)
Then, even then, He is blessing us!
And in the world, (when we don't know what is happening)
He is the One we can trust!
Glory to God! He is doing something new,
Wonderful works hidden from our view!
Glory to God! All He holds within His hand
He unfolds in his good plan!

31 HUMPTY DUMPTY SAT ON A WALL

On a class trip to Smith Island the sixth graders were immersed – quite literally – in marsh muck, bay breezes, and watermen's ways. They kissed a fish, tossed crab pots, and paddled their canoes all around the tiny town of Tylerton, population 56. Each day ended with a time of reflection, the whole group gathered sleepily around a flickering lantern, while each person shared thoughts of significance related to the day's activities. The Chesapeake Bay Foundation educators who prepared and taught our wild and whacky lessons were eager to tell me what a remarkable group they found our students to be.

"We see hundreds of kids go through these programs," they told us, "but this group is unique. First of all, we've never had kids sing a blessing like that – it was beautiful! Blew us away... And, they did the best reflections we've ever heard. Amazing..."

You can believe I was blessed to hear these kind encouragements. Of course, the trip wasn't all wonder and glory. There was, as I have mentioned, marsh muck. There was also the night that one of our sleep talkers solemnly intoned (at midnight): "Humpty Dumpty sat on a wall." (A long pause ...) "Humpty Dumpty had a great fall..." (And another long pause ...) "All the king's horses, and all the king's men" (silence, as I contemplate) "Couldn't put Humpty together again." I have never heard such a sober and articulate recitation of this particular piece of literature. It was a completely new way to think about Humpty.

Evidently, C.S. Lewis also found the story of Humpty Dumpty to be food for thought. In his essay entitled "Miracles" from the book *God in the Dock*, Lewis uses the tragic tale to illustrate the limits of science when attempting to explain the universe and its existence. He says:

The story told by modern physics might be told briefly in the words "Humpty Dumpty was falling." That is, it proclaims itself an incomplete story. There must have been a time before he fell, when he was sitting on the wall; there must be a time after he had reached the ground. It is quite true that science knows of no horses and men who can put him together once he has reached the ground and broken. But then, she also knows of no means by which he could originally have been put on the wall. You wouldn't expect her to. All science rests on observation: all our observations are taken during Humpty Dumpty's fall, because we were born long after he lost his seat on the wall, and we shall be extinct long before he reaches the ground... From the very nature of the case, the laws of degradation and disorganization which we find in matter at present, cannot be the ultimate and eternal nature of things. If they were, there would have been nothing to degrade and disorganize. Humpty Dumpty can't fall off a wall that never existed. (p. 34)

Recently, a group of parents and teachers spent some time engaging with Lewis's thoughts on what physics, philosophy, and faith can contribute to our understanding of the universe and its existence. We explored his "Humpty" metaphor by means of seminar discussions similar to those we use in teaching the students. Multi-layered, open-ended questions shared in small group settings led to stimulating conversation and challenging exchange of ideas. Students are taught to approach literature, scripture, works of art, and big ideas by generating and engaging with "discussible questions," responding respectfully and thoughtfully to the statements and observations of their peers. These seminars make no room for unsubstantiated claims, or unsupported opinions. Part of the challenge is to maintain fidelity to the text given, and to be prepared to defend one's position.

As our sixth graders departed Smith Island on the ferry back to the mainland, one of the Chesapeake Bay Foundation teachers accompanied us. She made a point of telling me once again how impressed she was with our students. "They are so inquisitive! You can tell they're used to thinking critically and asking thought-provoking questions. You can tell they're accustomed to making connections and diving right in to authentic dialogue on complex topics. This group is truly unique in those qualities."

Well, that was certainly great to hear! We are thankful to the Lord for the liberty He gives us to guide our children in seeing life from a **B**iblical worldview, in **R**elationship with the Creator and His world, using **I**ntegral curriculum which invites them into **E**xperiences of His Truth and Grace – a BRIE-filled Redemptive Education!

32 WIND FROM THE SEA

A special exhibit at the National Gallery of Art highlighted paintings by Andrew Wyeth. Titled "Looking Out, Looking In," the paintings all featured windows, often only a single window, with a notable absence of human figures.

The most famous of these "window" pictures, "Wind from the Sea," is typical of many Wyeth interiors: a shabby room, chipped wood sill and fading walls, a cracked window shade partially obscuring light, tattered lace curtains – all speaking of neglect and decay. Outside the window, we see a verdant forest, a grassy meadow through which some car or truck has left its tracks. We see only a hint of water that must be "the sea"; a broad sky. There is a marked contrast between the landscape and the gray room.

However, the curtains are not hanging limp, as one might envision them in such a state of abandonment. Wyeth explains:

> That summer in 1947 I was in one of the attic rooms feeling the dryness of everything and it was so hot I pried open a window. A west wind filled the dusty, frayed lace curtains and the delicate crocheted birds began to flutter and fly... I drew a very quick sketch and had to wait for weeks for another west wind for more studies.

Despite the circumstances described by the artist, when looking at this painting a viewer experiences a sense of coolness, a lively breath of oxygenated air infusing refreshment into the stale room. Curtains hanging limp with dust for decades suddenly billow in animation. Patterns long undiscerned emerge to dance and delight the eye. The effect is one of quiet restoration, a peaceful lifting of the heart.

Andrew Wyeth does not make religious claims regarding his art. Much of his work conveys brooding meditations on mortality, an existential angst familiar to most artists of the twentieth century. Nonetheless, we can find that "all things are His servants" and that we can profit devotionally from paying attention to this profound painting.

Look for those items in the picture that reflect the "hand of man": the fabric, walls, window frame, as well as the tracks left in the grass, all demonstrating the fate of human endeavor, an "absence" in the midst of merely human action. Look, then, for those things that reflect the "Hand of God": trees, sky, grass, water, and (most wonderfully!) wind. These are things which bring life, refreshment, vitality to human endeavor, to human action – they reflect a Presence most powerful in redeeming all things.

Thank you, Andrew Wyeth! Thank You, Lord! God uses the skillful work of Wyeth to encourage us as we tackle tough tasks of home and school. Reflecting on this painting invigorates our energies in participating with the "breath of God" to lead our children in their learning – what a privilege!

As we present to the Lord the works of our hands, our hearts, our minds, He promises to bring them to fruition for His purposes. We can entrust all things – all human endeavors, all human actions, all of our undertakings – to Him, knowing that His Spirit blows like a wind in and around, over, under and through our homes and school communities as we seek and desire *His* glory, *His* praise.

33 COWS AND CLOUDS

The second-grade girl was given a list entitled "Dairy Cows." It included the Guernsey, the Jersey, and the Brown Swiss, among others. "Children, please learn the names of these dairy cows," her teacher instructed. And so she did. That's why, nearly half a century later, I could reference "the Guernsey, the Jersey, and the Brown Swiss" with confident alacrity: I was that second-grade girl. What a wonderful thing it has been to know, with certainty, the names of these gentle breeds of dairy cows! I've never used the information once in my whole life.

I also know by heart the names of several varieties of clouds: the stratus, the cirrus, and the cumulonimbus. These were likewise acquired in my second-grade class at the Rose Hill Elementary School in Alexandria, VA, anno domino 1964. While it happens that I have found more practical use for this category of information, I recall no instructional activity connecting the various white streaks and cottony poofs depicted and labeled on the poster in our classroom with anything we might actually have expected to see in our very own skies, above our very own playground at school. Nevertheless, I memorized joyfully, finding pleasure in the powers of my intellect as recognized by the 100% on the top of my cloud test and the privilege of being the student chosen to carry a platter of our just-made butter (spread on Saltines) down to the Principal's office. (Joey and Karen were not chosen.) I have absolutely no recollection of the Principal herself (himself?) but you can be sure I have never forgotten how to be successful in school: Memorize the cows. Memorize the clouds.

Sometimes I wonder, though, what might have occurred if my teacher had said something like this: "Please use colored pencils on white paper to create a scene in which we see at least two varieties of dairy cows, and at least two types of clouds. Then, find a partner, and see if you can identify each other's cows and clouds." I just wonder – I can't help myself – I wonder if Joey, or Karen, for that matter, might also have found some success. After all, Joey was known for his artistic ability (although he always made a jumble of words, saying inventive things like "Jernsey" or "Brown Gurney.") And Karen – well, everyone knew that Karen was Not Smart and could not learn things like the names of the dairy cows or the various types of clouds. I don't know how or why we all knew this, but while never discussed, it was never contested.

What might have happened if Joey and Karen were partnered with the Brilliant Ones, and tasked with generating interesting questions we might like to ask about dairy cows or clouds? What might have happened if Joey and Karen (and the Brilliant Ones, for that matter) were given lumps of white playdough and asked to make cirrus clouds? What if Joey and Karen (and the Brilliant Ones) were told to make up riddles on the topics of cows and/or clouds, to share with the kindergarteners? Or what if Joey and Karen et al had been armed with masses of beautiful books, from which Joey would glean all the best info on the Guernsey – then share it with his peers, while Karen would become the local expert on the Jersey – and share that with her peers, and some other good soul made responsible for the bounty pertaining to the Brown Swiss? Or – joy! – what if the whole class had been taken to see and smell and touch and inquire of the Guernsey, the Jersey, and the Brown Swiss cow? I imagine that Joey and Karen and everyone else would have experienced something like "success in school" if our teacher had known to teach us in this way.

That was then; this is now: We want to have a thinking school, filled with thinking children who, if tasked with the learning of cows and clouds can not only memorize their marvelous names (shall we put them to music? make them into a chant? or create a scramble/unscramble puzzle of their respective letters until we can spell them properly and never forget them half a century later?) but can also delight in describing their colors, or demonstrate by their own warm breath on a cold window pane how a cloud is formed, or identify those threatening cumulonimbus in time to run in from recess, or explain to some interested party how the Guernsey and the Jersey differ, or the merits of cheese that has been made from the milk of the Brown Swiss.

34 MONTY ROBERTS,
THE REAL "HORSE WHISPERER"

As a thirteen-year-old boy sometime in the late 1940's, Monty Roberts was tasked with helping to round up wild mustangs in rural Nevada. The work was grueling and required every ounce of energy the boy could muster. In the lulls between roundups, Monty spent hours simply watching the horses run. Later, as an adult, he devoted seven years to living among them, carefully observing their interactions, fascinated by their "language": a cocked ear, a lowered head, an averted eye, a particular stance. Immersed in the complexities of the mustang community, he began to discern the effects of subtle exchanges he previously had not noticed. He began to understand the relationships within the herd, and between different herds. He began to understand the mind of the mustang, in its native setting and apart from any human interventions.

This long attentiveness bore fruit as Monty developed a method for training horses which relies solely on skillful use of the language he calls "Equus." Rather than employing the traditional method of "breaking" a horse (a term he eschews), Monty "speaks" to the horse, asserting his dominance without violence of any kind, convincing the horse to "join up" with Monty's "herd."

Monty's success in training all breeds and types of horses eventually led to his production of a video training series, two volumes of which are entitled "Join Up" and "Follow Up." It is fascinating to watch this master trainer communicate with any horse and eventually effect its willing cooperation. The equestrienne Queen Elizabeth was so intrigued by Monty's approach that she invited him to come and train her as well as those who handle her horses. He conducts training seminars and demonstrations all over the globe and speaks not only to would-be trainers but also to those who work with troubled adolescents, prisoners, and children with disabilities such as Asperger's. Many of the principles he discovered in his work with horses are seemingly universal in their effectiveness. The leaders of one elementary school were so impressed with Monty's insights that they designed their school culture and curriculum to incorporate these principles.

When a teacher loaned me her copies of the video training series, I expected to be interested because of my love of animals. However, Monty's story continues to surprise me with intriguing ideas and reflections I had not anticipated. His story raises so many questions!

Are any of our thirteen-year olds entrusted with such adult responsibilities as helping to round up wild horses? What would happen if they were? What would have happened if his parents (or the legal system) had determined that this activity was too risky, too dangerous for a child?

Did Monty's parents worry that he was too obsessed with horses? Did he appear "well rounded"? Did anyone exert effort to get him involved with other interests? What would have happened if they had?

What transpired in the years between his adolescent introduction to horses and his adult decision to spend seven years observing horses? What kept the interest and the dream alive? How did he justify his perpetual involvement with horses?

What did it look like when a teenaged Monty was watching the horses run? What did it look like when, as an adult, he observed the horses for seven years? Did he have any assurance ahead of time that this activity would result in a career?

Monty and his wife, a sculptor whose favorite subject is the horse, raised their own three children and 47 foster children as well. What did they learn from the horses that so equipped them for their work with children?

Could Monty's parents have predicted that their child's excessive interest in horses would someday take him to Buckingham Palace? Could they have guessed that he would be a hugely successful businessman, conducting workshops and giving lectures worldwide, and producing a bestselling video series?

Many of us are devoting time and thought to the development of curriculum for young adolescent students. As we purchase books, write thematic units, organize workshops and otherwise chart the course, we find the story of Monty Roberts to be a compelling one. It prompts us to ask: How might we make room for individual students' dreams and passions to unfold while studying algebra, chemistry and Beowulf? How can the adults in our learning community facilitate our children's ability to hear God's calling for their lives? How safe is "too safe"? How risky is "too risky"? What must we consider "imperative"? What might we consider "optional"? What cues do we take from the students? How do we train their minds for action? How do we disciple them to be joyful followers of the living God? How will we keep the whole person in view as we instruct, challenge, encourage and exhort?

I am a great fan of adolescents. They teach us to dream big dreams, to have high ideals, and always to be ready for action! Let's covenant together to pray for them, for those who will teach them, and for God to unfold *His* dreams, *His* plans in the hearts of our sons and daughters!

35 MY LIFE FOR YOURS

In Willa Cather's insightful novel, *Death Comes for the Archbishop,* she describes her main character, the young priest Jean Marie Latour who is lost in the New Mexico desert during his attempt to reach his new parish. Cather says, "His manners, even when he was alone in the desert, were distinguished. He had a kind of courtesy toward himself, toward his beasts, toward the juniper tree before which he knelt, and the God whom he was addressing."

I have found this description an intriguing one. I have been discussing it and its implications with our children in Chapel each morning. I asked them, "How can I demonstrate a kind of courtesy toward myself? What could that possibly mean?" The children told me: *You can take care of your body by eating right, and not doing bad things to it, and by getting exercise.* "Why should I do that?" I asked. *"Because God made you!"* Together we read from I Cor. 6:19-20, "Do you not know that your body is a temple of the Holy Spirit who is in you, whom you have from God, and that you are not your own? For you have been bought with a price: therefore, glorify God in your body."

We went on to discuss other forms of having courtesy toward oneself – and forms of discourtesy, too! When we say things like, "I'm so stupid!" or "I can't do anything right!" or similarly self-disparaging things, we are actually dishonoring someone whom the Lord created, whom He treasures, and for whom He has wonderful plans! Self-respect, when coupled with humility, honors the God in whose image we are made.

We were all quite touched that the priest, Latour, showed "a kind of courtesy toward his beasts." During Wilberforce Week, we had already noted that in an era during which harsh treatment of animals was not uncommon, Wilberforce established the first Society for the Prevention of Cruelty to Animals (SPCA). He saw this as an important facet of his quest to affect the "reformation of manners" (by which he meant the transformation of his culture to one that held virtue in high regard.) The children were eager to share what they knew about how to care for animals. Some were surprised that God's word also addresses this issue in Proverbs 12:10, "The righteous man has regard for the life of his beast."

Students could spend the entire year considering how to have courtesy "toward the juniper tree" as they study principles of godly stewardship of the land. They can plant the school garden with native species, learning why they are beneficial and how to cultivate them effectively. They can continue to learn the names of many trees, and how to identify them in the field, along with wildflowers, grasses, and other plants.

I pointed out that there was one category not mentioned explicitly in the description of Latour, but that which we could infer from the others. The perceptive children were quick to point out that, of course, we should have courtesy toward other *people*, as well as towards the flora, the fauna, and ourselves! Elisabeth Elliot tells us that courtesy is a way of saying, *"My life for yours"* – that every time we put the interests of another before our own interests, every time we serve someone else before serving ourselves, every time we take a moment to notice what another person might need or want, it is a way of laying down our lives for one another. It is a kind of "death" – a kind of sacrifice, and one's life is comprised of countless such acts of courtesy with each decision to put others first. God Himself tells us in Matthew 25:40: "Inasmuch as you did it unto the least of my brethren, you did it unto Me." This astonishing statement gives us the key to how we can have "a kind of courtesy" even toward the High King of Heaven who created us all.

C.S. Lewis tells us *"You have never met a mere mortal!"* This principle serves as the foundation for our high regard for children, who for most of their lives will be our peers, not our inferiors, and whose destinies are eternal! God clearly charges us, however, with the duty and privilege of setting them on the right road, prayerfully surrounding them with the resources likeliest to help them know and love God and walking with them on the journey. As teachers and as parents, we model for our young disciples patterns of speech, action and attitude in our interactions with them, with one another, with the unbelieving world, with God's creation, and with God Himself.

36 DRAGON-SLAYER!

Two summers ago, during a graduate course at Covenant College, my professor stopped me in the middle of my sentence. "Forgive me for interrupting," he said, "I can't help but notice that you always refer to your class as 'the children' rather than 'the students' or 'the learners.' Is there some significance to this?" We proceeded to have a fascinating discussion on the topic, and I have continued to think about his question.

I believe there *is* a deep significance in naming this group of young people "the children" instead of "the students" or "the learners." While the children at school are certainly students, and are certainly engaged in the process of learning, these things alone do not define them. They are also explorers, observers, adventurers, doubters, disciples, athletes and artists, sinners and saints. They are sisters and brothers and nieces and nephews – daughters and sons, neighbors and friends. They are boys and girls.

One day, some first graders and I did some singing about dragons. It brought to mind an essay I wrote some years ago, when I had enough mother-years under my belt to realize that an evolution had occurred in my child-rearing philosophy. This realization significantly impacted my approach not only to parenting, but also to teaching. I offer it as a little piece – a tiny little piece! – in our own Heroic Quest to nurture the uniqueness of every child. After all, we are not merely dealing with "students" or "learners" – no! Some of them are *dragon-slayers!*

"Dragon-slayer"

Mothers, your sons were born to slay dragons. God made them of that stuff that seeks out dragons, and woe to the woman who fails to find legitimate dragons for her sons to slay!

When I was the mother of only one small girl, I had a comfortable, pious theory: we would not play with toy guns. When I was the mother of one small girl and one very small boy, that theory was blown to bits in the face of this reality: every stick, every block, every benign plaything of any sort was transformed in the fist of my male toddler into a Weapon of Destruction.

No, you can't blame TV - we didn't have one. No, his daddy did not have guns, or knives, or any of those deadly items a child might want to pretend he owned. This cherubic, mild-mannered baby became overnight the Defender of All - or the Enemy of All; it varied.

And you cannot attribute this to mere personality. My two sons are as different in nature as ginger and cream. But both are dragon-slayers.

Now I say this for one reason only: You simply must provide a dragon. For one boy, it's the opposing soccer team. For another, it's a mountain to conquer on his bike. Your boy needs to fall into bed at night completely spent from the day's battle. His armor is off, his weapons laid aside, and now he sleeps, knowing he has fought the good fight.

A word of caution: Do not think you can bring the placid dragon home, and present him to your son with a polite introduction. No, you must hide the dragon just around the corner from his room. It must seem to your son that his mother never dreamed there was a dragon in her house! Let him discover it with a shout as he pounces upon the foe. (The dragon must not smell faintly of your perfume.)

I think now you are ready. Yes, there is a certain degree of risk. A boy's dragon may be messy. It may demand long hours of his day and more of his mind than his math does. But think of this, please: You do not want to be the only dragon your son can find to fight!

37 A PLAYFUL CURRICULUM: PART ONE

A Vision with a Task: Christian Schooling for Responsive Discipleship edited by Gloria Goris Stronks and Doug Blomberg, while no longer in publication (but available online) guides the reader through thought-provoking chapters posing significant questions: *How do we get from vision to mission? How do we forge a community for learning? How **do** we learn? How do we **know**? How do we think about curriculum? How do we decide **what** to teach? How do we decide **how** to teach? How do we evaluate student learning?* and similar considerations. The book's title reflects its commitment to Christ-centered education with its goal being students' "responsive discipleship" to the Lord Christ.

In the chapter "How do we think about curriculum?" two parallel approaches to viewing curriculum are described. One consists of the triad *Play, Problem-Posing,* and *Purposeful Responding.* The other consists of the correlating points of *Immersion, Withdrawal, and Return.*

To consider just one pair of these points, during "Play" or "Immersion," students are given the opportunity to interact in unstructured or gently guided experiences with objects, ideas, materials, content, books, artworks, music. In the chapter section entitled "A Playful Curriculum," the editors explain:

> We learn as we rest in the coherence of things, as we allow ourselves to move freely (either relaxedly or intensely) among its various components. We come to know people, organizations, living rooms, dogs, language, by our ongoing exposure to them, if we are sensitively open. The curriculum should allow ample opportunities for this 'playing around with creation.' In educational terms, we may think of it as *broadening* experience. (p. 201)

This material provides us with plenty to explore, analyze, evaluate, and plan for as we reflect on the rhythms of our own homes and classroom lives. One teacher, realizing that her usual entry point to a lesson was that of "Problem-Posing" decided to employ "Play" as a fresh approach to curricular material for her students. Another observed that the math curriculum seems to be organized around a similar cycle, including lots of hands-on work with concrete objects, puzzles and projects, practice with problems and finally, stepping back to explain one's thinking. The "broadening experience" gained during "Play" leads to a multilayered and sophisticated understanding of concepts, rich in meaning. It's not just fun and games!

In a lecture by Dr. Douglas Tallamy, professor and Chair of Entomology and Wildlife Ecology at the University of Delaware, he explains that when children have access to natural spaces, such as meadows, they play with the myriad things they encounter there: insects, worms, plants with intriguing seedpods or comical "faces," the soil itself with its varying textures. They know the smell and feel of the living things in which they are immersed; they sense themselves to be a part of the meadow and its inhabitants. In a typical suburban yard, however, with suburban grass covering the tidy lawn and its unvarying landscape, preceded by pesticides that kill the bugs, and non-native plants which cannot support local wildlife, there is nothing to play with. The children go elsewhere.

However, where home and school promote and allow it, I have known children to become old friends with the spiders, the crickets, the geese and the worms. I have known a child so familiar with the ways of bees that she could catch a sleeping bee in her nimble fingers on a chilly morning and deliver it safely to the classroom bug jar with nary a sting. There is no shortcut to that familiarity! She had spent many, many hours perfecting her technique through the course of many, many mornings. The scientific names for her learning activities might be "observation" and "testing of hypotheses." To her, it was "playing with bees." (Is there an adult among us who would not have shrieked, "Don't touch the bees!"?)

(I'm reminded of a comment overheard on the playground once: a child's voice casually remarking to her friends, "I think it's time to stop putting the guinea pig down the slide." I wonder – I'm afraid to even think – what observations led her to that conclusion!)

38 A PLAYFUL CURRICULUM: PART 2

Adam receives the Breath of God and becomes a living being. Before he even opens his eyes, that first deep inhalation yields fragrance: grass, fruit, flowers, perhaps the warm scent of cattle or the earthy musk of moss. Do his fingers touch the feathery foliage of an asparagus fern? Do they rest on a sunbaked stone, smooth by a stream? Do his ears rattle with the laughter of a pileated woodpecker?

He opens his eyes: Wonder! Wonder! This Eden! This paradise of Earth! And the Glorious Presence!

He runs – for miles and miles and miles. His whole being sings with the music of the spheres. For long ages he watches the dancing of stars. He studies ripples on the surface of lakes; he learns the texture of feathers and fur. He discovers grapes with explosions of sweetness, the spicy sassafras root, winterberry, peppers. He handles the newborn world in its loveliness: fearless, harmless, curious, glorious himself in the light of the Glorious Presence!

Then Adam is given a project to do. God assigns him a task, requiring thought and observation, creativity and astute discernment. God poses a problem: Who are these creatures? What are their names? What will you call them, Adam? That one with the back full of spikes – who is he? And that one, with turquoise tail feathers and a crest on his head: name him, please. What about that large striped one – orange, black, deeply purring and whiskered: yes, "Tiger" is good. And "armadillo" and "blue bottomed baboon" and "wolf spider" and "sloth" and on and on.

Adam does not neglect his assignment – he responds with joy, intelligence, strength. The challenging task is an honor, a privilege, a sacred responsibility. As he names each animal, he rejoices to hear his Creator's enthusiastic endorsement. Deep is his satisfaction, deep is his pleasure: he is doing what he was created to do, participating by God's directive and by His invitation, in this very good work.

Well, wasn't God clever? Way back there in Genesis, He created the pattern of "Play - Problem-Posing - Purposeful

Response" just as we can read about in Stronks' and Blomberg's book *A Vision with a Task*. God immersed the new humans in the setting which He had prepared for them. He surrounded them with plants, animals, objects, weather, experiences of all kinds – each reflecting in some way the character and creativity of their Maker.

Then, God required Adam to step back, take stock, consider, pronounce. The "problem" God posed was perfectly designed for Adam, requiring intelligence, observation, decision-making capabilities, speech. In the process of his obedient response to this challenge, Adam further expanded his intellect and understanding. He was qualified to participate because God had both equipped him and commanded him to undertake the task. As he participated, he became increasingly knowledgeable and more fully equipped for future undertakings.

This is our model for education. We carefully prepare: classroom, curriculum, schedule, school culture. We make lesson plans; we buy materials; we arrange desks; we paint walls; we clean whiteboards; we craft policy; we read books. We invite the children in: Explore! Examine! See, touch, listen, smell, taste, handle, observe, experiment, play!

This immersion then leads to some "problem posing": What do you think would happen if? ... Why did it do that when you did this?... How could you make it?... Where might we find those?... What will it cost if?... Who is the most courageous character?... When did that happen before?... Do you know if it's true?... How do you know that it's true?... What would you do if?... Why? Why? Why?

In Socratic seminar, in Narration Stations, in math "explorations," group projects, inquiry science, reading assignments – we ask the children to respond. We ask them to show us, tell us, convince us, write it, sing it, act it, calculate it, design it, build it, explain it.

As they respond – which God designed them perfectly to do – they continually grow in knowledge, in skill, in relationship with one another, the world, and God. Call it what you will: "Immersion – Withdrawal – Return" or "Play – Problem Posing – Purposeful Response" – God has set the pattern. He has shown us a wonderful way to teach our children, by helping them to explore God's world and discover their place in it.

39 ALMOST DROWNING

Due to the inconvenient activities of my nose, sinuses, throat and chest these past several days, I have spent a lot of time reading at home. Unlike the writer of Ps. 131, I have been considering things "too difficult for me." A Tolstoy essay entitled "Are the Peasant Children to Learn to Write from Us? Or, Are We to Learn from the Peasant Children?" has largely baffled my brain. I think, however, I have gotten the gist of at least a few of its several main ideas. If I have understood him, Tolstoy maintains that:

- At its best, education is the quest to find the balance and harmony among truth, beauty, and goodness.
- Education is largely a matter of removing hindrances from and providing catalysts for a person's interior growth and development.
- A true teacher demonstrates humility in spending more time listening, questioning, and learning from students than in speaking, telling, or instructing those students.

However much of Tolstoy's genius remains inaccessible to me, I still walk away from that essay with plenty to digest, to consider, to examine critically and finally, to implement.

I have also been deeply immersed (almost drowning!) in Jeremy S. Begbie's book *Theology, Music and Time*. Almost drowning, I say, because every sentence is so intellectually challenging for me, so densely packed with academic vocabulary and concepts unfamiliar to me that I have to break the text into bite-sized phrases for analysis if I hope to glean any understanding from it at all. The entire first chapter is Begbie's thorough explanation of what he will and won't be attempting to assert throughout the rest of the book. In laying this foundation, he alludes to and quotes from such myriad scholars who have evidently spent their lives exploring "theology, music and time," or perhaps "sociology, music and time," or even "psychology, music and time" that his invitation to my meager participation in the conversation is daunting, to say the least.

Nevertheless, Begbie frequently assures me in his introductory chapter that "no particular musical expertise is required to read this book." I believe him. I am reading his book. And if I gain no more (due to my own limitations) than the ideas expressed in the first and last sentences of this introduction, he has still given me a great deal to ponder. He says: "My guiding conviction in this book is that music can serve to enrich and advance theology, extending our wisdom about God, God's relation to us and to the world at large. I hope to show this with particular attention to that dimension of the world we call 'time.'"

He finishes with:

> ...my hope is that at the very least the reader will conclude that music, so often thought to be at best half-articulate and at worst corrupting, has significant potential to help us discover, understand and expound theological truth, to the advantage of theology and the deepening of our knowledge of God.

Less instructive for me are statements such as the following:

> He (referencing the musicologist Nicholas Cook, in a footnote) attacks the idea of 'private consciousness' as a bourgeois social construction, but the same could be said of his conviction that 'human consciousness is something that is irreducibly public,' a belief which he thinks can pull us back from the abyss of extreme relativism, saving us from a 'pessimism' about understanding music and using it as a means of personal and social transformation.

Phew.

You see what rich waters I am swimming in! Thus far (I have reached page 52) I have been leaping behind Begbie's speedy boat, awash in the wake of his brilliant logic, gasping for air, and occasionally catching a golden fish - for example, I read (and even comprehend) several sentences whose point turns out to be that the three notes played in, say, a C major chord can each be heard distinctly as individual notes, but also in unity, as a single chord, thus illuminating the concept of the Trinity: distinctly Three, yet One. No individual note displaces or is displaced by the other two; all three are present in one "sound." (Begbie's more recent book, *Resounding Truth*, first introduced me to this idea, in a format more readily absorbed by the novice.)

Sometimes we ask our students to consider matters "too difficult" for them: the variety of explanations of Genesis' creation accounts; evaluations of issues in contemporary culture; the reading of challenging texts, as in sixth-grade students' assignments in the Pulitzer Prize-winning book *Beautiful Swimmers*, which was not written with children in mind. Kindergarten and first grade students learn stories from Shakespeare; nine-year olds memorize a C. S. Lewis poem entitled subtly "On a Theme from Nicolas of Cusa" (huh?) and learn to make connections between courage, sacrifice and liberty. We know that in these ambitious endeavors, there will be quite a lot that does not get grasped, understood, or retained. But -- as in my own ambitious endeavors in reading -- a few "golden fish," a few concepts and relationships newly uncovered to the inquiring intellect, will be valuable food for thought, "money in the bank" for future investment, or treasures to gaze on eternally.

40 WHAT MAKES YOU SAY THAT?

Recently, I was talking with a mom who shared that in trying to cultivate communication with her introverted child, she has to invest two and a half hours of just "hanging-out-doing-nothing-special-time-together" before his responses move beyond, "Mm-hmm," "Uh-uh," or "I don't know." While initially tempted to feel impatient, eventually this wise mom realized that two and a half hours of quiet availability, with no press of expectation, no intensity of attention, are what it takes to convey to her introspective offspring her authentic readiness to share whatever he wants to share, whether companionable silence or soul-baring. Her demonstrated willingness to enter his silence is exactly what enables him to believe her interest in his soul-baring. But she has to be willing to receive either one - after two and half hours of what seems like "nothing much."

With my four children, all it took was my turning out the light and sitting on the side of their bed for a few moments. The "goodnight routines" were not complete without the story, the prayer, the kiss, the attempted parental departure, and the urgent, "Wait, Mommy – can I tell you something?" Sure, it was sometimes an ingeniously manipulative plot to further forestall inevitable bedtime – but often it was the opening line of a six-year old's tale of woe, a ten-year old's account of adventure, a twelve-year old's ponderings of perplexities, or a fourteen-year old's existential angst. If I had not lingered, I'd have missed the whole story.

Some of you, however, cannot relate to either of my anecdotes because your child is perfectly happy to talk to you, to anyone, on any topic, on no topic whatsoever, all day long, all night long, in the car, in the store, in the church pew, in the yard and (so you hear) in class at school and you have no sympathy either for me or for the Wise Mom in my first account above. Stream-of-consciousness is *your* child's modus operandi and you would like to encourage me and other mothers of introverts to thank our lucky stars for a moment's peace and quiet. You wouldn't mind a sentence or two of substantive dialogue, but the seemingly endless and possibly meaningless monologue coming from the back seat is about to drive you nuts.

Parents aren't the only people facing challenges in this department. Teachers spend many hours every day either trying to get children to talk or trying to get them to stop talking. Both can be a problem.

But whether you find yourself teetering on the brink of two and half hours' companionable silence or teetering on the brink of a tucked-in-child's bedside story (again) or teetering on the brink of sanity because your child will not curtail her cheery if indiscriminate prattle, you may appreciate the counsel of the good folk from the Harvard Graduate School of Education. In their fascinating book, *Making Thinking Visible: How to Promote Engagement, Understanding, and Independence for All Learners (2011)* authors Ritchhart, Church and Morrison advise the use of a key question in the quest to stimulate and elevate both thinking and dialogue with children. This powerful question may transform "Mm-hmm" into elaboration, "uh-uh" into explanation, and "I don't know" into exploration.

Are you ready for the Powerful Question? (Drumroll...) It is, as you might have guessed from the title of this article, the simple query:

"What makes you say that?"

I add to this two other effective tools for drawing out thinking and dialogue with children (and other people):

"Can you tell me about that?"

and the innocently uttered phrase:

"I wonder ..."

When Melissa says, "I hate this stupid book. I'm not gonna read it," you quietly ask, *"What makes you say that?"*

"It's stupid. I hate it. Ms. Fribble is making us read it and I hate it."

"Can you tell me about that?"

"The other kids can read it but I don't know what the words say. It's stupid."

"I wonder if Ms. Fribble has some other books you might read?"

"Well, she said we have to read it."

"Hmmm... I wonder what she would say if you told her the problem."

"Well, probably she would help me find a different book."

"What makes you say that?"

"Because she helped Lisa find a different book yesterday."

"Can you tell me about that?"

"Lisa was mad and Ms. Fribble said what's wrong Lisa and Lisa said this book is too hard and Ms. Fribble said really and Lisa said yes and Ms. Fribble said let's see if we can find one that is just right for you and Lisa said OK."

Aha.

When Theo predicts during a science demo, "It's going to sink! I know it's going to sink in the water!" you extend his thinking and assess his real understanding by asking, *"What makes you say that?"* If he says, "Because everything sinks in water!" you can follow up with, *"Tell me about that."* If he says, "Well, at least rocks always sink in water," you are then in a position to hand him a piece of pumice and ponder, *"I wonder if this one will sink?"* and then, *"I wonder why it didn't?"* and then, *"I wonder how we could find out about that?"* and when he looks it up in his rock book and shouts, "I know why!" you then say, *"Can you tell me about that?"*

Some of you may be bothered right now. You're saying, "Yes, yes, yes ... that's all very well. But what about ... *you* know..."

Ah, yes.

For the parents of the cheery Constant Commentators, let me just say that while use of these questions may not curb excessive talking, it is *almost* guaranteed to elevate its content to something you can tolerate for an hour at a time and possibly even enjoy. After that, and a goodnight kiss, you might just have to turn off the lights and run.

41 SOUL SNACK

Susannah plays middle C. One hundred three children hum to match the note. Most of them are watching me – that's good, because they know when to cut off the sound at my signal. They are watching my hands; they are taking a breath; they sing!

They sound like angels. Yes, some of the voices are more of a "joyful noise" variety than a "lovely and melodic" variety – but all are singing God's word with God's people and to me, they sound like angels!

> *"I will lift up mine eyes to the hills –*
> *From whence cometh my help?*
> *My help cometh from the Lord*
> *Who has made heaven and earth,*
> *Heaven and earth!*
> *He will not suffer thy foot to be moved;*
> *He who watches over thee will not slumber,*
> *He who watches over Israel will not slumber*
> *nor sleep." (Ps. 121:1-4)*

"Can anyone find some synonyms in there?" I ask. Many hands go up, so many that I allow the children to shout them out.

"Slumber and sleep!" they all holler.

"That's right! Now – can anyone think of any other synonyms for those words?" One by one they come up with synonyms: snooze, doze, rest, conk out.

"When someone translates a text from another language, it's important for the translation to accurately convey the exact meaning of the original. The Bible has had many different translations from the Hebrew and Greek in which it was first written. Even though the translators are all trying to make it accurate, they often choose different synonyms for the original words." I read Ps. 121 from the

NIV, the NAS, the ESV and the King James, on which their song is based.

"This next version, though, is not a translation. Eugene Peterson, the author of this book, *The Message,* wanted his readers to know that he was *not* trying to give an exact translation but rather his own paraphrase of the Bible. Who can help us remember what it means to 'paraphrase' something?"

A sixth-grade girl reminds us that "paraphrase" means "to put in one's own words." We talk for a minute about why Peterson might have wanted to do that, and how the product differs from a translation. Then I ask the students whether they might like to offer their own paraphrase of Ps. 121.

Plenty of hands go up. The first child says, "When I have a problem, I talk to God about it. He will take care of me!" Another student adds, "You don't have to look to the mountains or something: God is the one who will protect you." A kindergarten boy reassures us with the reflection that even when *we* go to sleep, the Lord never dozes off or takes a nap.

"Does anyone here know someone who needs help from the Lord? Maybe some of us need His help and protection, too! Let's whisper to the Lord the names of people who need Him to watch over them, even while they are sleeping!" For a few still moments, all we can hear are the hushed whisper sounds of our intercessions.

Our morning Chapel only lasts for about fifteen minutes. But those minutes are packed full of music, theology, listening comprehension, history, vocabulary, public speaking, and prayer! That's a good "brain food breakfast," a good "soul snack" for our students before they go on to the math and phonics, the reading and writing, the collaborative work and the calculations of the day.

42 WONDER AND WORDS

Poet and author Suzanne Rhodes recently spoke to our students about how she discovered, as a small girl, the powerful connection between wonder and words. She described wandering down to a small stream whose waters stirred in her such a deep joy and sense of God's presence that she wrote her very first poem in praise of it. Through the years Suzanne continued to find rich significance and blessing in the still surface of a lake, the tumbling riffle of a creek, or the ever-returning waves of the shore where she now resides. She encouraged our students to pay attention to the things in God's world which delight them – a cocky crow, an odd-shaped shell. She shared with them considerations of how to keep the "creativity stream" flowing.

Here is her list:
- Live in the vine. If you live in a vine, Jesus Christ, you will always be reaching, budding, flowering, fruiting. You will also accept pruning as necessary so that you can be more fruitful.
- Try to see everything as if for the first time, as if waking up on Christmas morning. Never lose your sense of wonder. "Oh Lord, how shining and festive is your gift to us, if we only look and see." (Mary Oliver)
- Learn to be silent. We are fully alive when we are listening.
- Think in metaphors and similes, for it is the language of God. A chili pepper looks like an elf's shoe. Blackbirds sitting on telephone wires look like notes of a scale.
- Learn words by learning worlds (Annie Dillard). Study the works of God and man.

- Practice your craft, don't just talk about it. Dance your dance, write your poem, sing your song. Do it for all of your days.
- Recognize that all we have, all we are, and all we own is a gift - the generous hand is God's.

After Suzanne shared at the chapel service, she spent the rest of the morning guiding the sixth-grade class in writing poetry based on items she had found on the beach near her home. They included shells (of course!), the eggs of a conch (when one broke, a hundred minuscule conch shells fell from it, each one tinier than a sesame seed!), sea glass, one half of a vertebrae (an animal's, I am sure!), and a broken pair of very large sunglass frames. The sixth and seventh graders walked their way through the process of observing, describing, naming, and making metaphors before embarking on a challenging assignment: Write a poem in which you are the "found" item, telling the story of how you came to be "lost at sea." Together we chuckled, gasped, and exclaimed in appreciation of each author's delightful and creative poem.

Suzanne's excellent poetry guide for students entitled *The Roar on the Other Side* is well worth the purchase. Some of the students have already concluded that poetry will be a lifelong pursuit for them. All have a better understanding and a deeper appreciation for God's gift of language.

Enjoy this poem Suzanne shared with us:

"Goldberg Variations on Summer Peaches"
Peeling peaches at the sink, smitten
by five suns bleeding at the center,
listening to Bach as the golden
rapturous juice throbs like music
in a robin's throat.

With dripping wrists I wave away
a fly drawn to the sweet spillage
and taste every ruby note as if God
himself were kissing me
in my kitchen.

43 TRUTH OR CONSEQUENCES

When I was in sixth-grade, I had a memorable experience with a Big Fat Lie. It was my own Big Fat Lie, and it came about because a report I had done at the extreme last minute was so embarrassingly subpar that I flushed it down the toilet before I even turned it in. This was a foolish action on several levels, not the least of which was the unwillingness of a written report to be completely flushed down a toilet. (At school. During snack break.) Yes, this was a foolish action and bound to present me with some unhappy consequences.

I would like to tell you that I confessed my misdeed, found mercy, and vowed never to deceive anyone again, nor flush large papers down toilets. However, this would not be true, and I certainly want to be truthful. The painful truth is this: I told a Big Fat Lie.

"Amy, where is your report?" I heard Mrs. Chiminera's voice come across the classroom through a thick and heavy hat of guilt that sat upon my pounding head. I had no plan. I considered myself a somewhat clever girl, but I had not been clever enough to actually make a plan, and so the Big Fat Lie began – so small a beginning, so seemingly small...

"A boy snatched it from me on the bus." (Perhaps you can already sense the unfortunate direction this would have to take.)

"A boy?"

"Yes. A... red-headed boy."

"Who was it?"

"I don't know."

"You don't know? Was he one of our students?"

"I don't know." (... thump thump thump thump – my pounding heart!!) "I don't think so."

And here a long pause... a long, long pause in which Mrs. Chiminera weighs the fact that I have been a Good Girl for as long as she has known me, something of a leader, never in trouble, and am

100

earnestly recounting a very dubious tale. The long pause combines with my mounting panic and the Big Fat Lie grows Bigger and Fatter. "He just got on the bus, and grabbed my paper, and got off!"

An even longer pause. This story cannot possibly be true, and yet ... I am taken to the office of the Head Mistress, a very proper and British Mrs. Fabris who always divided truth from error. She asked me sensible questions: Did he get off immediately or at the next stop? How old was the boy? Do any of the other children know him? Did you tell an adult as soon as you could? Why did you wait the whole morning before telling Mrs. Chiminera? and on and on the dreadful interview went. I cannot even tell you how I devised my ridiculous answers. I couldn't keep track of my ridiculous answers. The grown-ups had to realize it was all a Big Fat Lie.

But you know, they never told me so. By some amazing grace, they did not look me in the face and cry "LIAR! LIAR! PANTS ON FIRE!" Whatever contortions we went through in our dialogue, somehow the end consisted of the understanding that I would re-do the report and turn it in the next day. I spent the afternoon and evening writing and illustrating the best report I could possibly produce, complete with a detailed map and my very best cursive using my excellent fountain pen with black ink. No points were taken off for a late submission; no one said, "Amy, I am sorry to say that I think you are telling us a Big Fat Lie"; no one ever mentioned it again and I think somehow I concluded (with relief, with immeasurable relief) that perhaps I was not going to die. But I never forgot the anxiety, guilt, stress and general misery imposed upon me by my Big Fat Lie.

Many years later, when I was introduced to Sir Walter Scott's insightful observation: "Oh, what a tangled web we weave when first we practice to deceive," I knew the truth of it. And so you will understand why I have a sympathetic bond with whoever the School Soap Bandit is.

Ah, so your children have told you! You've already heard about the School Soap Bandit? Then you know that s/he has left his/her mark now several times in the boys' and girls' bathroom, with a large soap puddle in the middle of the floor, or a drizzle of soap across the toilet seats ...

But no one has "fessed up." Someone is clearly telling me their particular version of the Big Fat Lie. I am very sorry for this child. I know every single one of our children, and they are all Good Boys and Girls and not one of them would do such a thing, except one of them has. Poor child! Poor suffering soul! Poor mischievous miscreant! I know how the burden of the Big Fat Lie weighs on the conscience. So – I am praying that this precious child will be able to do what I never did with my Big Fat Lie: face the facts, tell the truth, take the consequences. May mercy triumph over judgment! For this is the Lord's way with repentant sinners of all stripes, including liars like me. ☺

44 SONG IN THE NIGHT

"Where is God my Maker, who gives songs in the night?" (Job 35:10)

At 3:15 a.m. last Friday, I was pulled out of a deep sleep by the sound of a melody coming from my clock radio. It was a melody played on a cello, with resonance that reached down into my dreams and brought me to consciousness. My usual method of waking is to notice my cat, Oscar, sitting on my chest with his paw on my cheek, pleasantly reminding me that it is time for a teaspoon of Little Friskies Whitefish and Tuna Pate. But even Oscar was asleep at 3:15 a.m. and he didn't lift a whisker when I got out of my bed.

I was on my way to a funeral in Ohio. In a journey familiar to many of you, the day would be spent mostly in airports. The significant event would be brief and intense. Dito Melvin, who died at the age of 28, was a gifted vocalist, a tenor whose singing friends would envelop us in the songs he had loved, while we sat immersed in melody, harmony, lyric and voice. We pondered mortality and immortality, their mysteries tumbling over one another in our hearts:

> *Deep calls to deep at the sound of Thy waterfall;*
> *All Thy breakers and Thy waves have rolled over me.*
> *The Lord will command His lovingkindness in the daytime;*
> *And His song will be with me in the night,*
> *A prayer to the God of my life! (Ps. 42:7-8)*

High Street A Cappella, the men's octet with whom he had sung, left an open place where Dito would have stood with them, and they sang one of his favorite pieces, in which the angel, Gabriel, is addressing a saint newly arrived in heaven:

"Set down, servant!"
"I can't set down!
My soul's so happy that I can't set down!"

The finger snappin', foot tappin' rhythm of this old spiritual lifted the hearts of the listeners and reminded us that we were celebrating a resurrection. No more encumbrance, no more dialysis, no more disease. It was a mingling of grief and jubilation, those odd companions who visit believers in times of bereavement. The paradox of simultaneous sorrow and joy brought waves of emotion which engulfed the congregation. It was as easy to laugh as it was to cry, as easy to praise as it was to petition.

As I lay gratefully on my bed that night, having safely returned from the chaos of airports, engine troubles, delays on the tarmac, missed connections, wrong directions and a funeral, I thought of Mary. What an incomprehensible jumble of realities the mother of Jesus had to bear! No sooner was she cradling her long-awaited baby than the prophet was exhorting her that this Child would cause the rise and fall of many, and that a sword would pierce even her own soul! Luke tells us, "But Mary treasured up all these things, pondering them in her heart." It would seem that throughout His childhood years, Jesus' mother and father had always to live within a mystery, in which blessing and bafflement, worship and wondering were constantly interwoven.

And so it is for us. Mysteries abound. Some, like shepherds dozing in dark fields, do not seek Him, yet they find Him. Some, like wise men, seek Him tirelessly, and they, too, find the Savior. Some, like Herod, only seem to be seeking, and they do not find Him. We live and then die; we die and then live. Into our darkness, He brings His light. He gives us songs in the night...

"I will remember my song in the night; I will meditate within my heart, and my spirit ponders..." (Ps. 77:6)

45 WAITING

We did not have long to wait. Two days after the official due date, six hours into the labor & delivery project, our newest little twig on the family tree had sprouted and was in our arms! We welcomed Vienna Jeanne Whitlock into the world on Dec. 9, 2013, having had our season of waiting brought to a swift culmination. *Gloria in excelsis Deo!*

Simeon, however, had to wait most of his multiple decades to behold the fulfillment of a promise made to him long before. Poet Luci Shaw begins her poem named for the old saint with these opening lines:

> *Expectant, though never knowing quite*
> *what he was watching for, the old man*
> *had waited out the years of a long life*
> *to be in the right place,*
> *at the right time.*

Because it was not possible for Simeon to know "what he was watching for," the old man had waited. And how did he manage to be "in the right place, at the right time?" Surely it was a matter of a long fidelity – the walking with holy expectation in the midst of the ordinary – an hourly obedience for decade after decade – the daily living out of devotion – while "looking for the consolation." Thus, was Simeon found to be "in the right place, at the right time." There it was that the Holy Spirit came upon him, filling his heart and fulfilling the promise.

And what a bittersweet promise it was! *"He would not see death before he had seen the Lord's Christ"* – and now, he had seen Him. In humble respect for the custom of the Law, without premonition of additional drama, Joseph and Mary had brought their newborn baby into the Temple to present Him to God. The Holy Spirit fulfilled His promise to Simeon, then filled Simeon's mouth with a promise to

Joseph and Mary – a bittersweet prophecy: Who could understand such a message? *Behold, this Child is appointed for the fall and rise of many in Israel, and for a sign to be opposed – and a sword will pierce even your own soul...*

So now, like Simeon, we wait. We wait for the promises of God to be fulfilled in our lives and in the lives of our children: *"And all your sons will be taught of the Lord, and great will be the well-being of your sons!" "Train up a child in the way he should go, and when he is old, he will not depart from it!" "See how great a love the Father has bestowed on us, that we should be called the children of God; and such we are!" "Behold, I am coming quickly, and My reward is with Me, to render to every man according to what he has done."*

We want to receive the promises of God! We want to be "in the right place, at the right time." We accomplish this just as Simeon did: we set our face to a long fidelity – we walk with holy expectation in the midst of the ordinary – we offer an hourly obedience, for decade after decade, if that's what it takes – we live out a daily devotion to Christ – and we look for the "consolation" to come, the un-grieving of every grievous thing, the un-weaving of sin and death and disappointment:

Behold, I make all things new!

46 DARKNESS AND LIGHT

Rembrandt Van Rijn, 17th century Dutch artist, is famous for his remarkable use of contrast between darkness and light. His paintings, drawings and etchings skillfully employ shading, white space, color and line to convey the light from a fire, the shadow of a fold of cloth, the depth of a cave. A series of copper etchings depicting Biblical scenes includes "The Adoration of the Shepherds, With a Lamp." As in all of the etchings, only thin black lines create the scattered hay, the weary mien of the Madonna, the respectful shepherd's doffed hat, the benevolent cattle bowing, and the bright halo of light emanating from a small oil lamp. The faces of every person in the picture are illuminated by that tiny flame. Rembrandt clearly says to the viewer: Here is Jesus – the Light of the World!

We have been thinking about darkness and light. This is a fitting follow-up to the fall's considerations: "the secret things" (which belong to the Lord) and "the things revealed" (which belong to us and to our children forever). We realize that what we are able now to know about God - His creation, His character, His kingdom – is a fraction of what there is to be known! He has sovereignly chosen to reveal to us whatever is at present important for us to know; the rest, He shrouds in mystery.

Wherever there is darkness, He Himself is "the light." We say, with Micah, "Although I walk in darkness, the Lord will be a light to me" (Micah 7:8).

The children have thought about varieties of "darkness" common to us all: sorrow, illness, confusion, fear, anger, sin. They have sung about "Christ, the Child born from the skies!" from contemporary poet, Luci Shaw's lovely work, "Night's Lodging," affirming that this Child brings His light to our "purple-patterned" lives, so "dappled with dark." As early as the 4th century, AD, the Greek bishop Synesius was writing:

In the Father's glory shining
Jesus, Light of light art Thou;
Sordid night before Thee fleeth, --
On our souls Thou'rt falling now...

Rembrandt's near contemporary, English poet George Herbert (1593-1633), wrote:

O Thou, whose glorious, yet contracted light,
Wrapped in night's mantle, stole into a manger;
Since my dark soul and brutish is Thy right,
To Man of all beasts be not Thou a stranger ...

May our Savior Christ – Jesus, the Light of the World! – be no "stranger" to us in this Advent season! Immanuel – "God with us" – bring Your lovely light to our every kind of darkness as we celebrate Christmas!

47 TO EVERYTHING THERE IS A SEASON

That's what we've been singing: "To everything, there is a season! There is a time for all good things..."

And, of course, it's true. As first grade students begin their formal education, they learn that there is a time for sitting, and a time for running – a time for "listening ears and hands" and a time to speak with a "leader voice." Meanwhile, second and third graders are discovering that there is a time to gather insects, a time to observe them, a time to read and write and talk about them, a time to release them. They see that the caterpillar has its time for wiggling in their hands, its time for eating voraciously, for spinning its cocoon, for transformation (while it looks like nothing's happening) through the quiet winter months.

The whole school population is thinking a lot about how to develop GRIT: Growth Mindset, Resilience, Initiative and Tenacity. There is a time for experiencing success and a time to learn from "good" failure. There is a time to bounce back from disappointments and a time to forge ahead with courage. Wisdom helps us discern when to take initiative and when to allow others to lead – when to persevere and when to yield. The Lord of all seasons is in our midst as we sow and reap, as we mourn and dance, as we try and try again, as we "let go and let Him" do His good pleasure.

All summer long, I watched the progress of the cornfields in Rockingham County. During rides in the country with my elderly father, who was visiting, we tracked the increasing height of the stalks, the emergence of ears, the browning of tassels. We marked the goodness of green and gold, each cornfield rich with metaphor about God's sovereignty, order and providence. My father travelled home before the green and gold became brown; just last week, the corn was harvested:

The corn is cut.

And now the stubbled field
may rest its weary roots, untroubled
by curtailment of its stalks,
endeavor brought to halt:
the job is done.

Now may the mice begin to glean;
and now allow the breaking down
of fallen fiber: tassel, leaf, and stem,
abandoned ear.

Now may the lovely land be left to dream,
the generous soil restored, the green
give way to brown,
the harvest in.

48 FAMOUS DONKEYS WE HAVE KNOWN

Unless you just happen to have been "in" on all our recent donkey discussions during Chapel each day, you would never believe the number of important lessons we can learn from such notables as Eeyore (*The House at Pooh Corner*), Puzzle (*The Last Battle*), and Nick Bottom ("A Midsummer Night's Dream")!

But your children can enlighten you. Go ahead, ask them! Ask, "What can we possibly learn from Eeyore??" and they will tell you: Choose cheerfulness! Try new strategies! If you ask about Puzzle, they will gladly exhort you: Don't let someone trick you into being disobedient! As for lessons from the unfortunate Nick Bottom, well – that one has a warning about trickery, too (as in, "Don't let anyone trick you into being too silly!").

I had the privilege of leading Chapel for many years. It always yielded my favorite sort of interaction: rich and joyful as together the generations meet to corporately consider scripture, song, and story. When it is well done, chapel can be the single most unifying part of a school's program, an acculturating practice by which the tone and framework are established for all the endeavors of the day.

Chapel should be an authentic instructional venue. It is not merely a nod in the direction of Christian tradition, but is, in fact, a complex and concentrated "class" during which we are doing many things at once: shaping a school culture that engenders both dignity and delight; building a common vocabulary (academic and otherwise); facilitating the development of relationship among children of varying ages, the varieties of adults who teach them, and our God; teaching a lot of people to sing; learning how to think; demonstrating an integral approach to organizing and delivering multi-disciplinary content from a biblical worldview – while attempting to model a range of instructional strategies for faculty and parents.

Creating a daily experience of intellectual, spiritual and emotional growth for this diverse group of learners is a challenge I embrace. The real work of preparing for Chapel launches several hours before I begin my commute to school each morning. As I immerse myself in God's word, meditating on a small portion of text and prayerfully considering it, I often find a theme emerging from that text for which multiple "connections" to previous considerations may be found. Donovan Graham observes in *Teaching Redemptively: Bringing Grace and Truth* to your Classroom, "As God spoke, all things entered a relationship with each other and were given a purpose."

The expectation of identifying significant "relationship" in all facets of education is also recognized in secular circles. In *Teaching as if Life Matters* by Christopher Uhl, the author asks, "Why this focus on relationship? It's simple! Everything that happens – from the level of cells that constitute our bodies to the mysterious workings of the cosmos that encompasses us – is a story of relationship."

Often, what Ms. Staples is teaching in her fifth-grade class connects to something Mr. Stewart is teaching in his Latin class and to something that the faculty are discussing in their meeting and to something the first graders are experiencing during recess and that they all connect with something conveyed in the biblical text for the day. We should not be surprised: after all, there is one Author writing His story in our midst and we will see the plot and characters developing if we are paying attention.

The Chapel experience is what educators would describe as a "biblically constructivist, collaborative learning activity." We give multiple people of varying ages and abilities the opportunity to serve in a role that learning theorist Leonard Vysgotsky identifies as the More Knowledgeable Other (MKO). While I might begin the morning's consideration in the role of the MKO, I swiftly hand it off to a student who can explain to the entire assembly what is meant when the story I've read tells us, "Jimmy, the little donkey of the Somme, was awarded the rank of corporal, and his chevrons mounted upon his harness." Our young MKO is able to help us understand the vocabulary corporal and chevrons, because he happens to be a military enthusiast. Earlier in the discussion, the humanities teacher served as the MKO by telling the rest of us about the Battle of the Somme. A sixth grader has already made a close guess about the meaning of "infamous" – as in "the infamous Battle of the Somme" – thinking, quite reasonably, that perhaps this would mean "not famous." A seventh grader offers the correction – "famous for a bad reason" – and so the many MKO's in our midst interact with the many listeners, and all are thinking together.

Donovan Graham asserts that an authentically Christ-centered approach to educating "... encourages us to have a living faith that takes knowledge gained in class and puts it to use for the benefit of humankind." And, since it doesn't hurt us one bit to learn from donkeys as well as from one another, please feel free to join us in discovering more useful lessons from "Famous Donkeys We Have Known"!

Don't try to take over the world
– Prince Rabadash (The Horse and His Boy)

Don't let too much Fun make you Foolish *– Pinocchio*

Help others as they have helped you *–Jimmy, little donkey of the Somme*

Tell the truth when someone is doing wrong *–Balaam's donkey*

Be ready to serve in new ways *– the donkey Jesus rode on Palm Sunday, who had never been ridden before.*

49 HURT NO LIVING THING

I love helping children explore God's world and discover their place in it. What a joy to lead children in their learning! However, it's a well-known fact among teachers and parents that we adults are always learning things from the children.

Some years ago, I learned something about worms. Second and third graders were singing a song based on Christina Rossetti's poem, "Hurt No Living Thing." The text of the poem is as follows:

> *Hurt no living thing:*
> *Ladybird, nor butterfly,*
> *Nor moth with dusty wing,*
> *Nor cricket chirping cheerily,*
> *Nor grasshopper so light of leap,*
> *Nor dancing gnat,*
> *Nor beetle fat,*
> *Nor harmless worms that creep.*

As I had done in other years, with other classes, I asked the children, "Which of these creatures is different from all the others?" No problem: "Worms!" Of course. Then I asked, "Why? What makes a worm different from all the other creatures named in this poem?"

I imagine you know what I was expecting. After all, these students had been studying insects since the first day of school! But not a single child said a word about insects. Instead, they thoughtfully made these observations:

The worm is the only harmless creature named in the poem. (This we discussed. I was a skeptic at first, but they made a strong case and persuaded me.)

- It has no legs.
- The worm is the only one that squiggles. (Closely related to #2)
- It has no eyes.
- The worm is the only one which can instantly change its size.
- It has no antennae.
- It has no wings.
- It's the only one that makes us say, "ew."
- Only the worm lives its whole life underground.

Now let me tell you, I have had plenty of opportunity in my life to have a good look at worms. Four children of my own, and countless other peoples' children have come running in my direction, with a squirming pink worm attempting its escape, while the children cry, "Look! Look! I got a worm!" So you understand, I have considered myself on familiar terms with worms.

But in all those years, with all those children, and all those worms, I had never once noticed any of the interesting distinctions listed above. It required the eyes of eight-year olds to open my eyes to the fact that the worm has no eyes. It was truly an intellectual exercise (led entirely by these second and third graders) to examine the statement, "The worm is the only harmless creature named in the poem."

Don't worry. We did not fail to conclude (in a backwards, but authentic sort of process) that the worm is the only one which is "not an insect"; but the conclusion was reached through a rich journey of discovery, fueled by the acute observations of some open-minded little children.

50 A "GRITTY" MESSAGE FROM A NAVY SEAL

I happen to be married to a man whose life goal is "to help people and change the world." This mission is both simple and profound. Being inspired to giving and serving in such a way as to fulfill that mission has certainly helped me and changed me, if not yet the world. Certainly, it contributes to my understanding and pursuing the mission of helping children explore God's world and discover their place in it.

I was further inspired this past week by reading the commencement speech given by Naval Admiral William H. McRaven, ninth commander of U.S. Special Operations Command, at the University-wide Commencement at The University of Texas at Austin on May 17, 2014, as reported on the university's website. He shared ten lessons from his training as a Navy SEAL. All of them employ powerful metaphors, and several need his accompanying anecdotes to be easily understood. However, the following three stand alone and merit the consideration not only of soon-to-be-grads, but also those of us who lead them.

> **If you want to change the world, start off by making your bed**. If you make your bed every morning, you will have accomplished the first task of the day. It will give you a small sense of pride and it will encourage you to do another task and another and another. By the end of the day, that one task completed will have turned into many tasks completed. Making your bed will also reinforce the fact that little things in life matter. If you can't do the little things right, you will never do the big things right. And, if by chance you have had a miserable day, you will come home to a bed that is made – that you

made – and a made bed gives you encouragement that tomorrow will be better.

If you want to change the world, find someone to help you paddle. You can't change the world alone – you will need some help – and to truly get from your starting point to your destination takes friends, colleagues, the good will of strangers and a strong coxswain to guide them.

Every SEAL knows that under the keel [of the enemy ship] at the darkest moment of the mission is the time when you must be calm, composed – when all your tactical skills, your physical power and all your inner strength must be brought to bear. **If you want to change the world, you must be your very best in the darkest moment**.

Thank you, Admiral McRaven! Only three from his list of ten – and plenty to work towards over the summer. Do your children (and you!) make your beds each morning? Such a little thing – such an excellent place to begin!

Are your children (and you!) cultivating relationships in which they can strengthen their own and others' "paddling" against the strong currents of contemporary culture? Take some time to hop in someone's "boat" this summer and join them in their journey. Facing some unanticipated "white water"? Invite someone to throw in their oar and be your paddling partner!

Are your children (and you!) refining those "tactical skills," that "physical power," that "inner strength" that will make it possible to shine in the "darkest moments"? View every small challenge your children face as an opportunity to help them strengthen those character "muscles" that will best equip them for life and for learning. To bolster your own skillset as parents hoping to cultivate "grit" in your kids, hunt down a copy of one or both of these excellent books: *Building Resilience in Children and Teens* by Dr. Kenneth R. Ginsberg, or *How Children Succeed: Grit, Curiosity, and the Hidden Power of Character* by Paul Tough.

Let's take to heart these final words from the Admiral: Changing the world can happen anywhere and anyone can do it!

51 NOT JUST A BAND-AID

Every mom knows that there's very little that a Band-Aid cannot cure. The kindergartener who comes tearfully in from recess with his invisible "boo-boo" will find a remarkable recovery with a brief application of a hug, a little prayer, and a Band-Aid. The robust fifth-grade student who "wipes out" playing soccer may be almost fully restored with a thorough washing of the scraped knees and elbows, a little antibacterial cream, and a lot of Band-Aids.

There's a lot that a Band-Aid can do.

But no one would be foolish enough to stick a Band-Aid on a broken bone, or a case of influenza, or an appendicitis. If one of those walked into the school office, anyone would know that a Band-Aid wouldn't do the job. A fracture, a flu, or an appendicitis need the work of a physician, some serious medicine, possibly surgery, and a good long recovery.

The same may be said for our nation's public schools. Diane Ravitch, educational guru who has labored long for the love of America's children and their academic well-being, bemoans the deeply diseased institution of the public school system. In her second-most-recent of many books, *The Death and Life of the Great American School System* (2010), Ravitch pleads for the restoration of the neighborhood school, which served for so much of America's history as a center of community life, a hub of society. She pleads for the schools to be released from their current obligation to play the impossible role of parent, police, physician, psychologist, social worker, and return to the task of being educators. Quoting W.E.B. Du Bois, she states "the only way schools can improve society is to make men more intelligent by teaching them academic skills. If they fail to do that, [Du Bois] warned, they will fail in all other functions 'because no school as such can organise industry, or settle the matter of wage and income, can found homes or furnish parents, can establish justice or make a civilized world'" (p. 285). Ravitch explains, "[While] schools can provide a route out of poverty for determined individuals, ... schools – no matter how excellent – cannot cure the ills created by extreme social and economic inequality. They cannot create jobs or repair broken families or end neighborhood deterioration or stop crime" (p. 286). Some may challenge her use of the word *"inequality,"* as *"impoverishment"* may be more to the point. However, with regard to public schools she rightly observes, "Education is a reflection of society. Education is integrally related to the society in which it is embedded" (p. 285). Can anyone question that American society is in a state of grave danger, and troubled by evidence of a deep disease? So also, then, are our public schools. We pray, and many of us serve, in the attempt to remedy its profound distress.

The cure cannot be found in a Band-Aid. It cannot be found in a Bible verse, either. A Christ-centered school, offering itself as one part of the prescription for healing and renewal our culture so desperately needs, cannot just do "business as usual" with a Bible verse stuck on. It must not merely be "traditional school" plus a little religion thrown in for good measure. A Christian school needs to courageously claim a wholly "other" endeavor: a Redemptive Education.

What *is* Redemptive Education? It is biblical – not just a Bible verse stuck onto its surface – but emerging from and reflecting a perspective that observes everything and everyone from this worldview framework:

- What was God's original intent? (for human beings, for art, for mathematics, for government, for society)
- Where, and to what extent do we see that original, good intent? (reflected in this historical person, this painting, this geometric proof, this country's form of government, this culture we are studying)
- Where, and to what extent do we see evidence of "the fall," of sin, of error, of a perversion or a brokenness? (reflected in this character, this sculpture, this hypothesis, this historical era we are studying)
- How is God calling me, calling us to participate in His redemptive work in response to our study of the above?

This is a Biblical Worldview. We see our children, our parents, our faculty, our board as beloved image bearers of Christ. We see our landlord, fellow Christian educators, the greater community and culture as being comprised of beloved image bearers, worthy of the compassion, love, service and prayers of God's people. We see all Truth as God's Truth (as per Augustine). We believe that "[T]he earth is the Lord's, and its fullness thereof, the world and all who dwell in it" (Psalm 24:1). We grieve that sin and error and wrongness not only make themselves known in the wicked world "out there," but also in the Christ-hungry souls of our own selves. We – the "we" of the world and the "we" of the Body of Christ – are wholly and desperately in need of His redemption. We cannot put our hope in a broken system with a Bible verse stuck on.

52 BEETLES AND BEETHOVEN

Most of you are not old enough to remember the Beatles in their early days. However, when I was a first grader at Rose Hill Elementary School in Fairfax County, VA, back in 1963 (half a century ago!!), the "talent show" that year featured not one but three groups of small boys in Beatles wigs, lip-synching such classics as "She Loves You, Yeah, Yeah, Yeah" and "I Want to Hold Your Hand."

A mere five years later, the Beatles had moved from writing lyrics about young love to making political commentary, singing:

You say you want a revolution,
well, you know ... we all want to change the world!

At the Center for Redemptive Education, well, you know... we do want to change the world! We want to help children explore God's world, not just memorize data about it. We want to help children discover their place in His world, not merely ensure that they "succeed" in the academic rat race out there. To do that, we need to be revolutionary educators – Redemptive Educators! Teachers and parents partner in labor and prayer, in order to equip our precious children to explore without fear, to take with them the tools and skills and attitudes that enable them to engage with the world, to see their Creator's reflection in each lovely thing, and begin to discover their own place in His plans.

This is a revolutionary idea, running, in many ways, quite counter to the prevailing educational currents of increasing standardization and measurement. How do we quantify a growing confidence? The cultivation of curiosity? Fidelity? Joy? There is no standardized test for these gifts of learning and of love. Along with instructing in academic skills such as multiplying fractions, naming states and capitals, and greeting one another with a hearty Latin "Salve!" we seek to arm our students with an eagerness for "The Heroic Quest," an understanding of their geographic and spiritual "watersheds," and the knowledge that this is our Father's world.

Beethoven, like the Beatles, was also a revolutionary fellow in his day. His final symphony, the ninth, shocked its 19th century audience in its catastrophic thundering of timpani, its confident departures from symphonic conventions, and the surprising inclusion of hundreds of human voices singing what we later would call the "Ode to Joy"– an innovation unheard of prior to this masterpiece of a master musician. Beethoven's theology reflected the Romantic influences of the era, but one recurring theme in this powerful choral component of the ninth symphony is the idea of joining hands and hearts with "Alle menschen! Alle menschen!" (all people) to forge a revolutionary bond of hope and endeavor. When "baptized" into a biblical worldview, we may see this bond as one reflecting the unity within the Body of Christ and in our school communities as together we answer God's call to educate our children. It is a revolutionary call – a call to Redemptive Education, marked with the unmistakable marks of both grace and truth.

This call is not only revolutionary but quite impossible – apart from the Source of that grace and truth. In the person of Jesus, His word, His Spirit, we have reason for our hope and our endeavor. For this reason, we not only work but also pray, asking for fruitfulness, blessing, protection and wisdom for every aspect of our ministry, here in the United States and around the world.

AUTHOR

Amy Imbody is the founder and director of the Center for Redemptive Education, a non-profit organization dedicated to the quest to align with God's design for teaching and learning. Author of *Gathering Seed, Little Levi,* and the award-winning *Snug as a Bug,* Amy writes, teaches, composes music, and leads little kids in her outdoor-based early childhood program, "Boots & Roots." Her books are available at Amazon.com and her poetry in various issues of *First Things* as well as *Cricket, Ladybug* and *Spider* magazines. Mother of four, grandmother of four, wife of the very nice Mr. Jonathan Imbody, and cat-lover of the rascally Jericho, Amy makes her home in Ashland, VA, with gratitude to the Creator for having made such a beautiful world.